# The Mystery Library

# Astrology

## Stuart A. Kallen

**LUCENT BOOKS**

*An imprint of Thomson Gale, a part of The Thomson Corporation*

**THOMSON**

**GALE**

Detroit • New York • San Francisco • San Diego • New Haven, Conn. • Waterville, Maine • London • Munich

On Cover: A sixteenth-century artist's depiction of the signs of the zodiac appears on a ceiling fresco in the Palazzo Ducale in Mantua, Italy.

LIBRARY OF CONGRESS CATALOGING-IN-PUBLICATION DATA

Kallen, Stuart A., 1955–
  Astrology / by Stuart A. Kallen.
    p. cm. — (The mystery library)
  Contents: The mysterious elements of astrology—Astrology, personality, and health—Astrology's influence on daily events—Forecasting and transforming the future.
  Includes bibliographical references and index.
  ISBN 1-59018-839-X (hard cover : alk. paper) 1. Astrology. I. Title. II. Series: Mystery library (Lucent Books)
  BF1708.1.K36 2006
  133.5—dc22

                                                                2005031110

Printed in the United States of America

# Contents

# Foreword

In Shakespeare's immortal play, *Hamlet*, the young Danish aristocrat Horatio has clearly been astonished and disconcerted by his encounter with a ghostlike apparition on the castle battlements. "There are more things in heaven and earth," his friend Hamlet assures him, "than are dreamt of in your philosophy."

Many people today would readily agree with Hamlet that the world and the vast universe surrounding it are teeming with wonders and oddities that remain largely outside the realm of present human knowledge or understanding. How did the universe begin? What caused the dinosaurs to become extinct? Was the lost continent of Atlantis a real place or merely legendary? Does a monstrous creature lurk beneath the surface of Scotland's Loch Ness? These are only a few of the intriguing questions that remain unanswered, despite the many great strides made by science in recent centuries.

Lucent Books' Mystery Library series is dedicated to exploring these and other perplexing, sometimes bizarre, and often disturbing or frightening wonders. Each volume in the series presents the best-known tales, incidents, and evidence surrounding the topic in question. Also included are the opinions and theories of scientists and other experts who have attempted to unravel and solve the ongoing mystery. And supplementing this information is a fulsome list of sources for further reading, providing the reader with the means to pursue the topic further.

The Mystery Library will satisfy every young reader's fascination for the unexplained. As one of history's greatest scientists, physicist Albert Einstein, put it:

> The most beautiful thing we can experience is the mysterious. It is the source of all true art and science. He to whom this emotion is a stranger, who can no longer wonder and stand rapt in awe, is as good as dead: his eyes are closed.

# The Planetary Rhythms

For thousands of years people have consulted astrologers to make sense of the past, learn more about the present, and peer into the future. In the twenty-first century the belief that the stars and planets influence the course of human affairs remains as popular as ever. Polls have consistently shown that nearly 100 percent of people in the Western world know their astrological sign. About one-third of the population believes in the tenets of astrology, and about 70 percent read the horoscopes printed in daily newspapers in the United States. Astrologers, both professional and amateur, cater to this interest by casting countless personal horoscopes every year.

Despite astrology's popularity, the basic concepts behind it have been challenged time and again by skeptics. H.J. Eysenck and D.K.B. Nias, for example, write in *Astrology: Science or Superstition?* that astrology "is an ancient superstition that survives only in the minds of suggestible people who lack any knowledge of scientific methods."[1] Believers, however, say that astrology has a record of accuracy dating back thousands of years. This claim is also challenged by critics.

## Science and Symbolism

Because of its elusive nature, astrology is classified as a pseudoscience because practitioners use scientific concepts to draw unscientific conclusions. The scientific aspects consist of mapping the exact positions of the sun, moon, planets, and constellations using complicated geometric formulae and a knowledge of astronomy. The unscientific side is the belief that each heavenly body has a mystical meaning and significance. For example, Mars, because of its red color, symbolizes such so-called hot events as war, aggression, and murder. The position of this planet—and the others in the universe—at the time of a person's birth is said to have a specific influence on his or her daily life, personality, and future.

*In this sixteenth-century print, Arabian astrologers examine the heavens.*

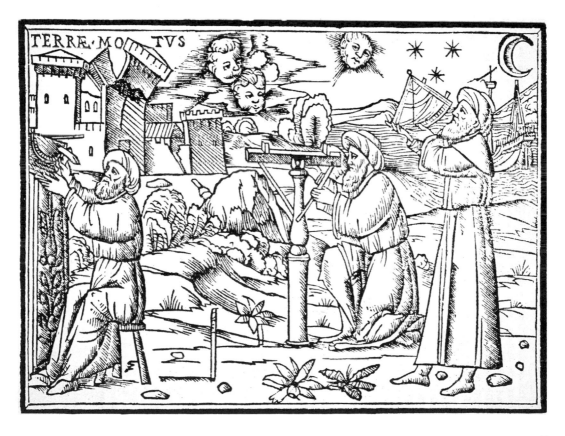

*Astrologer Joan Quigley displays some of the charts she uses in making her predictions.*

Although astrology is mathematically complex and intricately symbolic, its popularity can perhaps be traced to the human desire to know what the future holds and how events can be influenced. For those who are confused over questions of love, money, health, life, and death, astrology can provide guidance, no matter how tenuous. For this reason, people consult astrologers to pick favorable dates for weddings, travel, and other events. They check their baby's birth chart to determine his or her future needs, and they consult the stars when struck down by sickness and disease.

## Believers and Skeptics

For those who believe, life can be guided by understanding the alignment of the planets and stars. Nonbelievers wonder how what they see as confusing and contradictory influences can really mean anything. In *Objections to Astrology*, Bart J. Bok and Lawrence E. Jerome hypothesize that people do not really believe, for example, that the position of distant Mars can predetermine earthly events. Instead, the authors write, in "these uncertain times, many long for the comfort of having guidance in making decisions. They would like to believe in a destiny predetermined by astral forces beyond their control."[2]

*The Roman soldier–poet Horace was skeptical of astrology.*

Another notable skeptic, the renowned Roman poet Horace, believed that people should concentrate on the present rather than worry about the unpredictable future. Writing in the first century B.C., Horace stated:

> Don't ask . . . what final fate the gods have given to me and you . . . and don't consult . . . horoscopes. How much better it is to accept whatever shall be, whether [the God] Jupiter has given many more [years] or whether this is the last one. . . . Be wise, [pour] the wine, and trim distant hope within short limits. While we're talking, grudging time will already have fled: seize the day, trusting as little as possible in tomorrow.[3]

Despite the advice of Horace, people will continue to look to the stars when earthly answers fail to solve intractable problems. They may not fully believe that the sun's position will help them pass a biology test or find true love, but a horoscope may help focus the mind and provide at least some answers where none were apparent before. As long as the world is filled with great uncertainty, millions will continue to consult the stars for the sense of comfort that a trust in cosmic forces gives them.

# Chapter 1

# The Mysterious Elements of Astrology

People have been casting horoscopes for thousands of years, and astrology is one of the oldest forms of study known to humanity. The concept of blending stargazing with religion, magic, and philosophy began many thousands of years ago, when the night was lit only by campfires and people lived in small nomadic hunting tribes. The main evening activity for prehistoric people consisted of closely studying the moon, planets, and more than two thousand visible stars as these bodies appeared to travel across the sky. These observations allowed even the most primitive cultures to gain a surprisingly comprehensive knowledge of celestial movements. One of the oldest human-made objects ever discovered is a piece of bone with the phases of the moon carved into it, apparently by a Cro-Magnon person over thirty-four thousand years ago.

In later centuries, people in China, India, Africa, the Middle East, Europe, North America, and elsewhere came to believe that the heavenly bodies, especially the moon, sun, and planets, were living gods who were responsible for all life on earth. Theses deities could see into the future and reveal messages about the destiny of mortals. As Peter Whitfield writes in *Astrology: A History*: "The sky and the natural world were pages upon which the gods wrote their decrees in mysterious but systematic language."[4]

Not all celestial signs were predictable, however, and unusual events, such as eclipses, shooting stars, and comets, were interpreted as omens from the gods. In ancient Egypt, scientist-priests called *ummanu* interpreted these harbingers along with the usual movements in the night sky. Using a

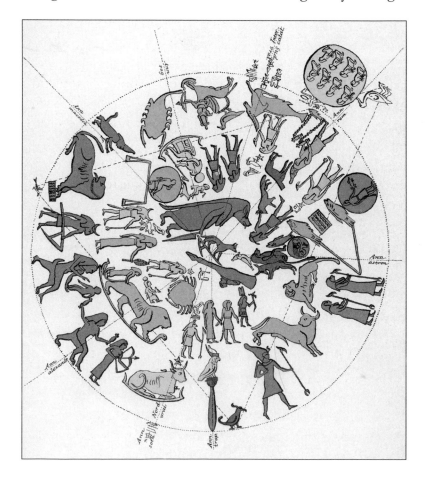

*This French engraving depicts the ancient Egyptian concept of the twelve signs of the zodiac.*

belief system that merged religious philosophy, observation of nature, and the science of astronomy, the *ummanu* divined the will of the gods and advised kings and nobility on matters of war, peace, royal succession, and government policy.

*An ancient Egyptian scientist-priest known as an* ummanu *used clay tablets to record omens from the gods.*

The observations and predictions of the *ummanu* were recorded on thousands of stone tables that listed omens and lucky and unlucky days. One such cuneiform text from 1700 B.C. told priests how to predict the coming year based on observations of the wind, clouds, and astronomy on the last day of the old year:

> If the face of the sky is dark [cloudy], the year will be bad.
> If the face of the sky is bright when the New Moon appears, and it is greeted with joy, the year will be good.
> If the north wind blows across the face of the sky before the New Moon, the corn will grow abundantly.
> If on the day of the crescent the Moon-god does not disappear quickly enough from the sky, disease will come upon the land.[5]

It remains unknown whether or not such predictions were accurate, although the Egyptians must have believed in the truthfulness of their prophecies or they would not have carved them into stone. The vague language of the forecasts is typical of many astrological prognostications, however. For example, it is unclear what is meant by the rate of speed at which the moon disappears from the sky. Similarly, while a moon that appears to set slowly might portend disaster, it was not unusual for ancient societies to be stricken with epidemics, crop failures, and drought regardless of lunar activity. Prophecizing adversity was, therefore, most likely a safe move for soothsayers, who could be dismissed, arrested, or even put to death for failing to predict calamities.

As the centuries passed, astrological predictions moved beyond wide-ranging events and became more personal. By the fifth century B.C., the Egyptians were using astrology to cast individual horoscopes, a term derived from the Greek word *horoskopos*, meaning observer of hours or seasons. In 450 B.C. Greek historian Herodotus described the Egyptian method of prediction:

> [The Egyptians] assign each month and each day to some god; they can tell what fortune and what end and what disposition a man shall have according to the day of his birth. They have made themselves more omens than all other nations together.[6]

Ancient horoscopes were much like those seen in newspaper columns in modern times; they were brief and tended to emphasize positive omens only. Then, as now, few astrologers wanted to upset believers by making predictions of poverty, sickness, and early death. For example, a horoscope from 235 B.C., cast for a child named Aristokrates, says that his "life will be regular, he will become rich, he will grow old, his days will be numerous. The place of Venus [in Taurus] means wherever he may go, it will be favorable to him. He will have sons and daughters."[7]

## The Earth-Centered Universe

Whatever the predictive value of heavenly movements, ancient astrologers based all their calculations on the false assumption that the earth was flat and located at the center of the universe. All celestial bodies, including the sun and moon, were thought to revolve around the earth.

*In this sixteenth-century celestial map, Earth is depicted as being at the center of the universe.*

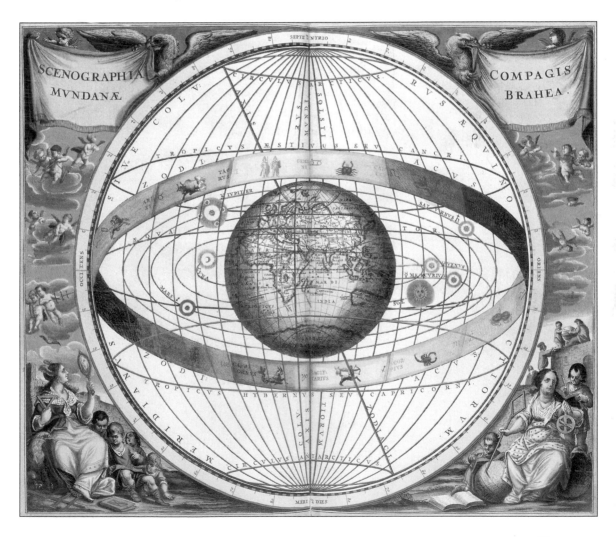

Using the model of the earth-centered universe, ancient astrologers developed a system that tracked the movements of what they called the "seven planets." These were the Sun and Moon and the true planets: Mercury, Venus, Mars, Jupiter, and Saturn. (Uranus, Neptune, and Pluto cannot be seen with the naked eye and were, therefore, unknown to the ancients.) In addition to the planets, astrologers named forty-eight groups of stars. These constellations re-sembled animals, people, and objects and also appeared to move across the night sky with seasonal variations.

In the ancient system, developed by the Babylonians around 400 B.C. and now known as the zodiac, the earth was thought to look like a flat board suspended in space. The sun was believed to travel around the flat earth from east to

*The signs of the zodiac appear around the edge of the face of this antique German clock.*

west in a 360 degree circle every day. Astrologers divide this path of the sun, called the ecliptic, into twelve sections, called houses, each taking up 30 degrees. Each house contains its own astrological constellation, that is, sign of the zodiac. The location of each constellation in the sky changes throughout the twelve months of the year as the earth orbits the sun. Therefore a person facing north at midnight will see Taurus in the center of the sky in February, and its opposite, Scorpio, in roughly the same place six months later in August.

## "Circle of Little Animals"

Astrologers relied on astronomical observations to develop the horoscopes. They noticed that the sun rises in front of each constellation for about one month. For example, twenty-five hundred years ago, when the sun rose on the first day of spring, March 21, the constellation Aries was behind it on the horizon. Thus people said that the sun was "in" Aries. About a month later, on April 21, the sun appeared to be rising in front of the constellation Taurus.

Around the fifth century B.C., the ancient Greeks began to call constellations of astrology the *zodiakos kyrklos*, or "circle of little animals," because they resembled recognizable figures. The Greeks also gave the zodiac the names by which they are known today. Aries the Ram and Taurus the Bull are followed by Gemini the Twins (appears in the sky May 21 to June 21), Cancer the Crab (June 22 to July 22), Leo the Lion (July 23 to August 23), Virgo the Virgin (August 24 to September 22), Libra the Scales of Balance (September 23 to October 22), Scorpio the Scorpion (October 23 to November 22), Sagittarius the Archer (November 23 to December 21), Capricorn the Goat (December 22 to January 20), Aquarius the Water Bearer (January 21 to February 19), and Pisces the Fish (February 20 to March 20).

The naming of the zodiac allowed the model of the heavens to be visualized and translated into drawings, paintings, and sculpture. By the third century B.C., Greek mathematician and astronomer Archimedes was using geometric calculations to build three-dimensional working models of the planetary system. Although they were based on the earth-centered model of the solar system, these replicas allowed astronomers and astrologers to calculate the positions of the moon, stars, and planets at any time past, present, or future. Because the movements of the stars could be mathematically predicted, it solidified the idea that the heavenly bodies could forecast the future.

Around 140 B.C., Claudius Ptolemy compiled astrological information from Babylonian, Egyptian, and Greek sources and wrote a book called *Tetrabiblios*. In the book, Ptolemy systemized and presented the information as the unified discipline of astrology. *Tetrabiblios* is still considered one of the most influential astrological guides in history. In the introduction, Ptolemy explains the workings of astrology:

> [If] a man knows accurately the movements of all the stars, the sun, and the moon . . . [why] can he not, too, with respect to an individual man, perceive the general quality of his temperament from the ambient [surrounding environment] at the time of his birth, as for instance that he is such and such in body and such and such in soul, and predict occasional events, by use of the fact that such and such an ambient is attuned to such and such a temperament and is favorable to prosperity, while another is not so attuned and conduces to injury?[8]

*Tetrabiblios* and other written texts allowed average citizens to learn about astrology and examine their personal

# Planets of Death

In ancient Greece, astrologers used Ptolemy's book *Tetrabiblios* as a guide to casting horoscopes. Near the end of the text, Ptolemy explains how various planets affect marriage, children, and material fortune. The following selection covers the many grisly ways the planetary influences may kill a person:

[If] Saturn holds the lordship of death, he brings about the end through long illness, phthisis, rheumatism . . . chills and fever . . . or hysteric conditions, and such as arise through excesses of cold. Jupiter causes death through strangulation, pneumonia, apoplexy, spasms, headaches, and cardiac affections, and such conditions as are accompanied by irregularity or foulness of breath. Mars kills by means of fevers, or intermittent at intervals of one and a half days, sudden strokes, hepatic [liver] conditions and those that involve the spitting of blood, hemorrhages, miscarriages, childbirth, [skin conditions], and pestilences, and such diseases as induce death by fever and immoderate heat. Venus causes death by stomach, hepatic, and intestinal conditions, and furthermore through cancers, fistulas, lichens, taking poisons, and such misfortunes as come about from excess or deficiency of moisture. Mercury portends death by madness, distraction, melancholy, the falling sickness, epilepsy, diseases accompanied by coughing and raising, and all such ailments as arise from the excess or deficiency of dryness.

*The ancient Greek scholar Ptolemy wrote a comprehensive guide to astrology.*

lives based on their horoscopes. This removed the predictive art from the exclusive realm of priests and kings. Hundreds of astrologers catered to the public, and the methods they used to cast horoscopes have changed little over the centuries.

## Challenges to Astrology

The Greek astrological system spread throughout the ancient world. However, the earth-centered universe that lies at its very core was challenged in 1610 when Italian astronomer Galileo Galilei published *Starry Messenger*. Based on Galileo's telescopic observations of the moon, the stars, and the moons of Jupiter, the book proved that the solar system is heliocentric—that is, the sun is at the center and the earth and the planets revolve around it.

Although the earth-centered astrological beliefs were proven to be flawed, Galileo himself believed in astrology.

*An astrologer in India explains her predictions for the outcome of an upcoming election.*

The year before he published *Starry Messenger*, the astronomer cast a horoscope for his patron, the Grand Duke of Tuscany, saying that the duke would lead a long and happy life. The prediction proved inaccurate, however, when the duke died suddenly two weeks later.

## Precession of the Equinoxes

Whatever the accuracy of Galileo's horoscopes, the heliocentric solar system is but one scientific problem that has challenged astrologers over the centuries. Another is referred to as the "precession of the equinoxes," a term that refers to the changing positions of the zodiac over time. This complicated astronomical problem is based on the fact that when the zodiac was first formulated by the Babylonians, the sun rose in Aries on the vernal equinox, or the first day of spring. Due to a slight gyroscopic wobble in the earth's rotation, it no longer does. While astrologers continue to base their horoscopes and predictions on the supposedly "fixed" position of Aries as the Babylonians saw it, the sun now actually rises in Pisces on March 21. Therefore, the signs named in ancient times no longer appear during the dates they are assigned today. This means that while someone whose birthday is in late March is considered an Aries by astrologers, he or she was actually born under the constellation Pisces.

Astrologers deal with this precession of the equinoxes in two ways. In India they acknowledge the problem and adjust their astrological readings to compensate for the reality of the shift. This school of thought is called sidereal astrology, and someone born on April 1 in India is considered a Pisces, not an Aries.

Most Western astrologers deal with precession of the equinoxes by separating the zodiac from the actual stars of the constellations. They base horoscopes on the way the signs relate to the turning of the seasons. This is explained by Dan Sewell Ward on the Science Versus Astrology Web site:

*An astrologer prepares an infant's natal chart based on the time of birth, determining at that moment the positions in the zodiac of the moon, sun, and earth, seen above, and of the other planets.*

Astrology simply does not in any shape, form, or fashion base its results upon the stars, the star backgrounds, or any of the constellations. These are simply names, and Scorpio could have easily been called the sign of "wild, sexy beast." Scorpio, on the other hand, *as a time of year*—when the days are rapidly growing shorter and the Sun approaching its winter solstice—does count for something. . . . Meanwhile, Capricorn is in the dead of winter and strongly encourages one to accept the boundaries and limitations of survival in such times. And so it goes. . . . An astrology based on one star, the Sun.[9]

By focusing on seasons—and ignoring the precession of the equinoxes—Western astrologers have not had to change or update their calculations for thousands of years. This has also allowed astrologers to avoid recalculating every horoscope and confusing the general public by assigning different astrological signs to millions of people. However, skeptics claim that astrologers' refusal to modernize their calculations means the very foundation of astrology is flawed. As Roger B. Culver and Philip A. Ianna write in *Astrology: True or False?*:

> That they have learned nothing basically new, seemingly does not bother the astrological community in the least. In fact, many astrologers take pride in pointing out that the essence of astrological thought has experienced little in the way of significant change for centuries. . . . Such cool confidence . . . has become the distinguishing characteristic of the pseudosciences. . . . [This] centuries-long immunity to the basic alterations of the "scientific" astrological view of nature can only be greeted with the greatest of suspicion.[10]

## Influence of the Sun

Few astrologers agree with the conclusions of Culver and Ianna, however, and continue to cast horoscopes using methods unchanged since the time of the ancient Greeks. When a baby is born, astrologers construct a birth chart to establish the locations of the sun, moon, and planets in relation to the zodiac at that moment. This is determined using planetary tables that list the exact positions of the heavenly bodies at a specific time. Such a chart might say that a child has the sun in Leo, the moon in Scorpio, Mercury in Virgo, Venus in Sagittarius, and so on. Another important factor used by astrologers is known as the rising sign or ascendant. This is based on the constellation that appears to be rising over the horizon at the moment of birth.

Most astrologers consider the purported influences of the moon, planets, and rising sign; however, the sun sign remains the most important. This may be traced back to the ancient Greeks, who believed that the sun was ruled by the god Apollo who traveled daily across the sky in a fiery chariot. Apollo was young, virile, and handsome, but could turn destructive when spurned. Based on Apollo's persona, astrologers believe that a person's sun sign governs his or her spirit, will, ambition, energy, and power. Conversely the sun sign may be linked with destructive traits such as egotism, arrogance, and pomposity. Best-selling author and astrologer Linda Goodman explains in *Linda Goodman's Sun Signs*:

> The sun is the most powerful of all the celestial bodies. It colors the personality so strongly that an amazingly accurate picture can be given of the individual who was born when it was exercising its power through the known and predictable influence of a certain astrological sign.[11]

The sun sign is also said to rule physical characteristics, career, health, and interpersonal relationships. These influences are determined by both the season in which the sign appears and the animal the constellation resembles. For example, Aries is associated with the first day of spring and its star pattern looks like a ram. Those whose sun sign is Aries are said to be like the spring season itself. That is, they act and think like youngsters their entire lives and are joyous like the spring flowers. They may be full of bluster like the March winds, and as energetic as the ram that the stars represent. On the negative side, they may be willing to butt heads like a ram fighting, or be as impulsive and impatient as children. Some astrologers even believe that those born under the sign tend to look like rams, with long noses, curly red hair, and strong jaws. They point to American president

Thomas Jefferson and Dutch artist Vincent van Gogh as two examples of the Arian facial type.

*Some astrologers say that Thomas Jefferson displayed several physical traits of the ram (inset), the animal associated with his sun sign, Aries.*

The influences of Taurus on a person are said to be similar to those of the bull seen in the constellation. People whose sun sign is Taurus are thought to be patient, stubborn, down-to-earth, and slow to anger but dangerous when provoked. Because the sign appears in late April and early May, those born under the sign of Taurus are said to enjoy bright colors similar to those of spring flowers.

Gemini people are said to have dual personalities like the twins seen in the stars. Although Geminis are considered highly intelligent as if influenced by two minds, their dual personality is said to make them fickle, contradictory, and flighty.

Those born under Cancer the Crab are compared to the oceans, feminine and receptive, but also powerful and life-giving. The masculine Leo is the opposite of Cancer. Like a roaring lion, a Leo can be loud, extroverted, egotistical, and proud. Virgo people are said to embrace the qualities of the all-knowing virgin goddess that symbolizes their sign. The Virgo may be wise, self-contained, critical, and analytical.

Libra, the only inanimate object in the zodiac, is represented by the scales of balance, and has a strong sense of

## "Not Witchcraft or Fortune Telling"

Within the astrologer community, some claim to cast amazingly accurate horoscopes that can reveal details of the future. However, as artist and astrologer Hans Bok writes in the foreword to *Heaven Knows What* by Grant Lewis, not all astrologers make such grand claims:

Astrology is a science, not witchcraft or fortune telling by supernatural means. If you want to know the exact number of children you are going to have, or the day a rich uncle will bequeath a fortune to you, go to a tea leaf or [Tarot] card reader. All that astrology can reveal to you is that certain specific factors—pleasant or unpleasant, constructive or destructive—will be in force (in relation to your self only) at any given time in your life.

Their nature and the departments of your life in which they will operate, can be named accurately, but astrology cannot predict any definite event, even though sometimes it seems to! It can tell you times when you might wish desperately to get married, and times when death might seem possible but it cannot state definitely that you WILL get married or die at those times. This is where your own free-will comes in. Free-will can't assure you that you'll be born undeformed or immune to circumstantial disease and warfare, but if you have reasonable intelligence you can, eventually, gain the proper perspective to cooperate with or defy the influences in force, capitalizing on them to the fullest when they are good, riding them out when they are bad.

justice and fairness. Scorpio appears in the fall and, like the autumn, represents life, death, and the circular march of the seasons. Scorpios can sting like the scorpion but can also be fearless, tenacious, and full of positive life energy. Those born under Sagittarius the Archer can also sting with words but, influenced as they are by the symbol of the arrow, Sagittarians are said to be travelers, friends who are straight and true, and people who can reach their goals quickly.

Capricorn is the sign often associated with the winter holiday season. Those born under Capricorn are said to love tradition and, like the goat that represents them, they can climb steep mountains to achieve their desires. Unlike the Capricorn, who prefers normalcy, those born under Aquarius the water carrier prefer to carry on with no restrictions in life. Lovers of freedom, Aquarius people can follow their own paths to become great artists or musicians. Finally, people born under Pisces the Fish, the last sign of the zodiac, are said to swim in the deep worlds of thought, imagination, and spirituality.

## Science Versus Sun Signs

For the millions of people who have faith in astrology, the characteristics associated with each sun sign are rarely doubted. For example, believers may refer to a friend, relative, or lover as the quintessential Pisces or Leo. Therein lies the mystery of astrology. To those who accept the basic tenets of the system, Aquarius acquaintances are indeed creative types and Scorpio friends can be described as fearless and vigorous. Such beliefs are known as empirical observations and are based on personal experience. However, these beliefs may be hotly contested by scientists. For example, a simple study conducted in the mid-1980s at Colorado State University challenged long-held astrological ideas.

The Colorado inquiry was based on the widely held view that Aries people tend to have red hair. Researchers questioned three hundred redheads at the university and asked them their sun signs. By simply dividing three hundred by twelve (for the number of signs in the zodiac), researchers expected to find an average of twenty-five redheads in each sign. This was very close to what they found. Twenty-seven redheads were Aries, twenty-two were Taurus, twenty-eight were Cancer, and so on. The sun sign Libra had the largest number of redheads, at thirty-four. However, according to *The Book of the Zodiac* by Fred Gettings, Libra people tend to have hair that is "yellow, or somewhat tending to flaxen."[12] Capricorns, who numbered thirty-one and made up the second largest number of redheads, are said by the same author to have dark hair. Commenting on the study, Culver and Ianna write, "There is no reason to believe that a statistically significant correlation exists between red-haired people and *any* of the sun-signs, including Aries."[13]

## The Moon and Planets

Astrologers seldom give credit to such studies and argue that such data is worthless because physical characteristics are sometimes difficult to classify. For example, a redheaded Libra might be what is called strawberry blond and thus conform to the flaxen definition, while a redheaded Capricorn might have dark hair with reddish tones. Moreover, if someone fails to conform to the typical traits of a Libra or Capricorn, believers point out that the positions of the moon, planets, and rising sign can also influence appearance, career choices, personality traits, and even long-term health.

The moon and planets are important to astrologers because each is said to have its own powers defined by Roman mythology. For example, the moon is believed to contain the qualities of the ancient Roman goddess Luna.

*The position of Mercury, named for the Roman god shown in this fresco, is said by astrologers to predict a person's ability to communicate, learn, and innovate.*

Since the moon controls the tides, its influence on a person is said to be cool, watery, and feminine, as opposed to that of the dry, hot, masculine sun. The position of the moon at birth is said to foretell a person's future behavior concerning relationships between mother and child. The moon's position also is believed to predict outward personality, sensitivity, temperament, and outlook on life.

Mercury, the planet nearest to the sun, is also characterized by Roman mythology. Known as a god who serves as messenger, Mercury is moreover identified as a brilliant inventor who flies through the air wearing a winged helmet and sandals. Because of these associations, the position of Mercury in a person's horoscope is said to forecast that person's future ability to communicate, learn, and innovate as well as experience travel.

Venus, the goddess of love and beauty, represents the feminine principle in a horoscope. This planet portends how a person will understand the feelings of others, express affection, and enjoy nature and art.

Mars, reflecting a light that is red, the color of blood, symbolizes Ares, the god of war. The influence of Mars on a horoscope is said to relate to masculine traits such as

# Testing the Claims of Astrologers

Dozens of scientific studies have been conducted to test the accuracy of widely held beliefs about astrology. Several are described by Andrew Fraknoi on "The Universe at Your Fingertips Activity: Activities with Astrology" Web page:

Psychologist Bernard Silverman of Michigan State University looked at the birth dates of 2,978 couples who were getting married and 478 who were getting divorced in the state of Michigan. Most astrologers claim they can at least predict which astrological signs will be compatible or incompatible when it comes to personal relationships. Silverman compared such predictions to the actual records and found no correlations. For example "incompatibly signed" men and women got married as frequently as "compatibly signed" ones.

Many astrologers insist that a person's Sun sign is strongly correlated with his or her choice of profession. Indeed, job counseling is an important function of modern astrology. Physicist John McGervey at Case Western Reserve University looked at biographies and birth dates of some 6,000 politicians and 17,000 scientists to see if members of these professions would cluster among certain signs, as astrologers predict. He found the signs of both groups to be distributed completely at random. . . .

Geoffrey Dean, an Australian researcher who has conducted extensive tests of astrology, reversed the astrological readings of 22 subjects, substituting phrases that were the opposite of what the horoscopes actually stated. Yet the subjects in this study said the readings applied to them just as often (95 percent of the time) as people to whom the correct phrases were given. Apparently, those who seek out astrologers just want guidance, any guidance.

aggression, ambition, power, and action. As Saffi Crawford and Geraldine Sullivan write in *The Power of Birthdays, Stars, & Numbers*: "Mars is the warrior god . . . [and] governs our survival instincts, whether we fight or flee. The [opposite] of Venus, Mars represents the male principle and is competitive, assertive, and ready for action."[14]

Because Jupiter is the largest planet, it is said to embody the traits of Zeus, the king of the gods. The planet therefore is believed to prognosticate how a person will be affected by religion, philosophy, justice, and spirituality.

Saturn, the most distant of the seven ancient planets, is said to be cold, slow-moving, and large. The Greeks associated it with Cronus, the fearful chief of a race of giants called Titans. Astrologers consider the planet's influences to be frequently negative and a harbinger of larger events in the world, rather than of individual actions.

## The "New" Planets

The seven ancient planets are considered the most powerful in a person's chart. In 1781, however, English astronomer William Herschel complicated the astrologer's task by discovering Uranus, a planet beyond Saturn. Since the huge planet, which takes eighty-four years to move through the zodiac, was discovered during the time of the American Revolution, astrologers claim that Uranus influences entire cultures and eras with disruptive changes. Uranus is also said to govern the degree of freedom and rebellion in the personality of an individual.

German astrologer Johann Gottfried Galle spotted Neptune in his telescope in 1846. Named after the Roman god of the sea, this planet, according to astrologers, influences the raw power of all humanity and the unconscious thoughts shared by all the world's citizens.

In 1930, astrologers were once again confronted with the task of defining a new planet's influence on the horoscope when Pluto, almost four billion miles from earth, was discovered. Astrologer Llewellyn George describes the workings of Pluto in *The New A to Z Horoscope Maker and Delineator*: "Pluto is called masculine, stern, somewhat inscrutable. . . . Invoked by or responsive to music, especially the kind of music called jazz. Pluto rules the underworld, the subconscious workings of the body, the fluxing influences, the contest between acid and alkali; the fusing actions."[15]

While George and others have been quick to assign new symbolism to the outer planets, scientists have used the discovery of Uranus, Neptune, and Pluto as more ammunition against astrology. Writing for the "The Universe at Your Fingertips Activity: Activities with Astrology" Web page, Andrew Fraknoi asks rhetorical questions about the outer planets in order to challenge astrologers:

> [What] happens to the claim many astrologers make that their art has led to accurate predictions for many centuries? Weren't all horoscopes cast before 1930 wrong? And why didn't the inaccuracies in early horoscopes lead astrologers to deduce the presence of Uranus, Neptune, and Pluto long before astronomers discovered them?[16]

## The Moment of Birth

Another issue skeptics use to question astrology forms the very basis of the natal chart: the moment of birth as defined by astrologers. In centuries past, birth times were based on estimations because accurate clocks did not exist. Without the correct time, however, the precise positions of the rising sign, moon, planets, and stars could not be accurately calculated. Today, time can be recorded with incredible accuracy but debate continues as to the exact moment of birth. Skeptic Robert Todd Carroll explains on the "Astrology" Web page:

Astrologers emphasize the importance of the positions of the sun, moon, planets, etc., at the *time of birth*. However, the birthing process isn't instantaneous. There is no single *moment* that a person is born. The fact that some official somewhere writes down a time of birth is irrelevant. Do they pick the moment the [mother's] water breaks? The moment the first dilation occurs? When the first hair or toenail peeks through? When the last toenail or hair passes [from the mother]? When the umbilical cord is cut? When the first breath is taken? Or does birth occur at the moment a physician or nurse looks at a clock to note the time of birth?[17]

*Discovered in July 2005, this new planet—as yet unnamed—is larger than the planet Pluto. Astrologers must determine the new planet's influence on the horoscope.*

As long as such questions remain unresolved, the scientific debate about astrology will continue. However, most of these discussions will likely be ignored as the general public is deluged each year with thousands of books, magazines, Web sites, infomercials, and study programs promoting astrology. With astrology's widespread popularity—and its grasp on the human psyche dating back thousands of years—there is little doubt that people will continue to look to the stars when seeking answers to questions concerning life, love, and the future.

# Chapter 2

# Astrology, Personality, and Health

The basic premise of astrology is that a person's personality and character are predetermined by the stars and planets at the moment of birth. Since human behavior is highly complex and often contradictory, explanations of it based on a natal chart can be complicated. The very makeup of a birth chart is also complex, consisting of a circle that represents the planet Earth. The area surrounding the circle symbolizes outer space and is divided into twelve sections, called houses. Each house is ruled by a planet and its corresponding sign. For example, the house ruled by Mars is associated with Aries; the house ruled by Venus is associated with Taurus, and so on. Astrologers use intricate mathematical formulas to calculate each planet's position at the time of birth and to determine the positions of the houses based on an individual's rising sign.

The astrologer can use this picture to calculate the aspects, or the angular relationships these bodies have to one another. Planets may be near one another (conjunct), or in opposition to each other (180 degrees apart on the chart). Other planetary aspects are sextile (60 degrees), square (90 degrees), and trine (120 degrees). While conjunct, sextile, and trine are considered harmonious, square and opposed aspects are thought of as unfavorable.

This intricate method for casting horoscopes allows the astrologer to explain the infinite varieties of human behavior when describing a person's characteristics. This may be seen in the horoscope of a person with a moon in Aries. According to Frances Sakoian and Louis S. Acker in *The Astrologer's Handbook*, this person is "volatile, emotionally impulsive . . . [and] can have sudden flare-ups of temper."[18] However, if the subject's moon is sextile to Venus in the chart, that same position is "favorable for all matters pertaining to marriage and home life. . . . [And provides] ease in social relations and communications"[19] for the subject.

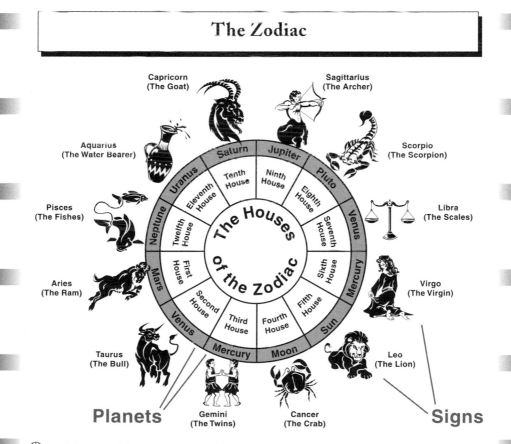

## The Zodiac

**Planets**

**Signs**

✸ Each house of the zodiac is ruled by a planet and its corresponding astrological sign.

# An Astrology Experiment

One of the main claims offered by astrologers is that they can identify personal characteristics of a subject simply by knowing his or her birthday. Skeptics claim, however, that these readings are often incredibly vague and could apply to any person. In *Bad Astronomy*, astronomy professor Philip Plait describes an experiment that demonstrates this point:

> The well-known skeptic and rational thinker James Randi (better known as The Amazing Randi) once performed an experiment in a schoolroom. The teacher told the class that Randi was a famous astrologer with an incredible record of accuracy. In advance the teacher had the students write down their birth dates and place each in a separate envelope. Randi cast a horoscope for each person in the room, placing them in the corresponding envelopes, which were then handed back to the students.
>
> After the students read their horoscopes, Randi polled them about accuracy. The majority of the students thought the horoscopes cast for them were accurate, and very few said they were inaccurate.
>
> But then Randi did an Amazing thing: he asked the students to hand their horoscope to the person sitting behind them (the students in the last row brought theirs up to the front row), and then read their neighbor's horoscope.
>
> The results were priceless. Surprise! Randi had put the exact same horoscope in each envelope. You can imagine the expressions of shock, then chagrin, then embarrassment that crept over the faces of the students. The wording Randi used was vague enough that it applied to nearly every student in the room. He used phrases like "you wish you were smarter," and "you seek the attention of others." Who doesn't?

*James Randi is a noted skeptic whose work includes debunking claims made by astrologers.*

To skeptics, the idea that a person can be volatile and temperamental while still having a happy marriage and easy social relationships seems contradictory. For those who believe in astrology, however, this is not problematic but rather shows the guidance value of a horoscope. An astrologer might interpret these aspects to say that the person with the moon in Aries could learn to tame his or her temper and so live to experience a happy marriage and full social life because of the moon's favorable aspect with Venus.

## A Scientific Study

Such wide-ranging interpretations of a horoscope are common, especially when astrologers consider all the other planets, ascendants, signs, and aspects. Consequently, the multifaceted method of determining a person's character has long defied scientific inquiry. Thus, anyone hoping to find hard evidence that two people with a moon in Aries might behave the same way would be confounded by the ostensible influence of other aspects of their birth charts. It has also been difficult to find objective astrologers or knowledgeable researchers who might be able to conduct such research. As Eysenck and Nias write: "Very few astrologers understand the requirements of science, and conversely many of the scientists who have become interested in this field have little understanding of astrology."[20]

This problem was confronted by French psychologist Michel Gauquelin, who began investigating statistical studies of astrology in the late 1940s. After discovering that earlier studies lacked proper research controls, Gauquelin set out to determine the validity of astrology using rigorous scientific methods.

Beginning in 1949, Gauquelin began collecting astrological data on thousands of notable people throughout Europe.

This information was analyzed to plot the planetary positions on their birth charts, which were then compared to the professions and personalities of the subjects. Gauquelin describes what he found on the "Is There Really a Mars Effect?" Web page:

> [I discovered] a series of highly significant statistical correlations between planetary positions and the birth times of eminently successful people. One of the strongest correlations I have observed is that sports champions tend to be born when the planet Mars is either rising or culminating [overhead at the meridian] in the sky much more often than it does for ordinary people.[21]

Gauquelin's findings showed that 22 percent of European sports champions were born with Mars rising or overhead. Since Gauquelin divided the sky into twelve sectors like a natal chart, the probability of Mars being in those two sectors of the sky is about 17 percent. Although only 5 percent more athletes had Mars rising or culminating, the difference is statistically significant because the odds are millions to one against it occurring by chance.

Gauquelin also discovered that the Mars effect applied to generals and physicians but not to painters and musicians. Other studies showed a correlation between the location of other planets and people in eleven different professions.

## Is There a Mars Effect?

Gauquelin published his findings in *The Influence of the Stars* in 1955, and his findings were quickly dubbed "the Mars effect." While the general public seemed to accept the findings, statisticians, astronomers, researchers, and scientists refused to believe Gauquelin's conclusions. The book set off a storm of controversy that raged for decades.

Psychologist Michel Gauquelin argued that sports champions such as skiers are more likely than nonathletes to have been born when Mars was rising or overhead.

In 1967, a Belgian group that strongly opposed astrology, the Committee for the Scientific Investigation of Alleged Paranormal Phenomena (known by its Belgian acronym CFEPP) set out to disprove the Mars effect. Members of the committee, including scientists, astronomers, demographers, and statisticians, gathered information about 535 sports champions. After studying the position of Mars in the athletes' astrological charts, researchers were surprised to find that 119, or a little more than 22 percent, were born when Mars was ascendant or at the meridian. However, CFEPP refused to release the results for eight years, attributing unspecified "demographic errors" for the outcome supporting the Mars effect. According to Eysenck and Nias, by not publishing its full report when its findings supported Gauquelin, the organization showed "bias, prejudice, and hostility."[22]

With the problem unresolved, another esteemed group of professionals decided to publicly condemn astrology. In 1975, *The Humanist* magazine published a short article called "Objections to Astrology" signed by 186 scientists, including 18 Nobel Prize winners. It read, in part:

> We, the undersigned—astronomers, astrophysicists, and scientists in other fields—wish to caution the public against unquestioning acceptance of predictions and advice given privately and publicly by astrologers. Those who wish to believe in astrology should realize that there is no scientific foundation for its tenets. . . . It is simply a mistake to imagine that the forces exerted by stars and planets at the moment of birth can in any way shape our futures. Neither is it true that the position of distant heavenly bodies makes certain days or periods more favorable to particular kinds of action, or that the sign under which one was born determines one's compatibility or incompatibility with other people.[23]

## Recreating Gauquelin's Study

Despite the scientific community's objections to astrology, another respected researcher attempted to verify Gauquelin's results. In 1976, American statistician Marvin Zelen asked Gauquelin to work with him to recreate Gauquelin's original study. The men decided to study the birth charts and astrological data of a control group of ordinary people, born at the same time and in the same places as a number of sports champions. It would be expected that the birth charts of the control group would show the rise or culmination of Mars in percentages similar to those of the athletes. For reasons unexplained by Gauquelin, however, this was not the case. He describes the results of the study, known as the Zelen test:

> I managed to collect 16,756 birth times of other people born within three days in the same places as 303 sports champions. . . . All the data was gathered in accordance with a very impartial procedure. . . .

# Careers in the Stars

By studying a subject's birth chart, astrologers believe they can give that person career advice. On the "Astrology, Hand Analysis, Management Science and Business Prospects" Web page, astrologer Yaschpaule offers an example of career advice based on astrology:

[The client asks] "What business suits me?" The astrologer says, "The planet Moon is well placed in Cancer in your birth chart. Your Ascendant is also in Cancer. So you will do well in the shipping business". . . .

The client now asks, "With which country shall I trade?" The astrologer replies, "As Cancer represents China, Holland, Canada or New Zealand, and it is in your Ascendant, you will do well by trading with any of these countries". . . .

The client now asks, "When shall I start the business?" By studying the client's birth chart, the astrologer can select the exact day and minute when the business can be launched.

The whole control sample gives an unequivocal answer to the Zelen test. The planet Mars is rising and culminating in greater proportion for sports champions than for the total of all other births registered on the same days in the same place as the champions. . . . [The] Zelen test report graphically illustrates the main empirical evidence.[24]

## The Controversy Continues

Although Gauquelin died in 1991, the controversy over whether the Mars effect exists lives on. People continue to question the accuracy of birth records, the methods for computing the position of Mars, and other methodology used in the study. In 1979, the magazine *Skeptical Inquirer* conducted its own study of American athletes and discovered that out of 408 champions only 55 (13.48 percent) were born with Mars in the key sectors.

Another contribution to the Mars effect controversy came from yet another study by CFEPP, conducted in 1996. After extensive tests the committee released its findings in a book, *The "Mars Effect": A French Test of 1,000 Sports Champions*, which stated: "We . . . conclude that the most careful analysis of 1066 French sports champions shows no evidence for the existence of the 'Mars effect.'"[25]

## Astrology in the Office

While the debate over planetary alignment and personal characteristics continues, astrology is making inroads in formerly forbidden territory. For example, there is a growing trend to use astrology in the workplace, a move critics strongly oppose.

Astrologers claim that horoscopes reveal personality traits that can help people work harmoniously, advance their careers, and learn how to deal with personnel problems at the office. As nationally syndicated columnist J.T. Ford writes in *Zodiac Manager*: "Executives are using astrology as a business decision-making tool. And the number of executives using it is increasing as business demands more accurate personal information in its move to hire and retain fewer, but more productive, employees."[26] European companies have led the way, and as many as 20 percent of large German, Swiss, and Scandinavian firms pay for astrological readings on executive candidates before hiring them.

In the United States, Richard Jenrette, chief executive of Equitable Insurance, credits astrology for his success. When Jenrette took over at Equitable, the staid Wall Street firm was nearly bankrupt. Within one hundred days, Jenrette was able to reverse the situation and turn Equitable into a Wall Street powerhouse. He attributes this turnaround to a belief in astrology that helped him make hiring and firing decisions based on a person's moment of birth. Jenrette claimed that he had to fire several executives who were stifling creativity because of the uniformity of their thinking. Although they knew they were hurting the company, they refused to resign. According to Jenrette, this is because they were born under Aries: "Because Aries are stubborn, they don't know when to quit— sometimes one should just walk away."[27]

Jenrette's analysis of Aries managers was likely derived from the beliefs astrologers hold concerning the work habits of people born under the various signs of the zodiac.

*As CEO of Equitable Insurance, Richard Jenrette used astrology in hiring and firing executives, a practice he claims helped him turn the financially ailing company around.*

*In this 1931 cartoon, a business executive consults his horoscope as he keeps track of a stock tickertape.*

With this as a guide, Jenrette might have deduced that Arians, in addition to being stubborn, can arouse intense feelings among coworkers that are either extremely negative or positive. This is said to cause a high turnover in staff when employees are unhappy with the pressure of working for an Arian boss who is unable to admit to his or her own mistakes and faults.

Astrologers believe they can help Aries bosses by providing them with methods to succeed despite alleged negative personal characteristics. For example, an Arian dealing with Jenrette, an Aquarius, can learn that Jenrette is said to possess strong ideals, prefer relaxed encounters over formal meetings, and value progressive thinking. Armed with this knowledge, an Arian can impress an Aquarian by conducting business in an informal setting, such as a restaurant or golf course. Teri King offers more counsel in *Business, Success and Astrology*:

Once business talk has begun . . . the [Arian] should give way to his enthusiasm, for [an Aquarian] will find it infectious. The Aquarian is idealistic and willing to help those he thinks are doing what they believe to be right. The financial side need not be discussed in depth; this character likes to show others that money is unimportant to him (though strangely enough, he will be one of the first to arrive when money is waiting for him.)[28]

While King's analysis might help in the short run, most astrologers state that an Aries/Aquarius partnership would not last long because both signs are said to personify strong character traits, egotistical impulses, and streaks of independence. By utilizing such information managers can make better decisions, according to Jenrette:

Astrology helps me (and can help you) understand and appreciate the differences in how each of us responds to events. . . . While I don't believe in poking into private lives unless work is being adversely affected, my lifelong fascination with what makes people tick, or 'Sammy run,' to use a few clichés from the past, has been my chief strength as a manager.[29]

## Planets, Partners, and Personnel

As a business executive, Jenrette may rely on sun-sign astrology to make personnel decisions, but professional astrologers use calculations that are much more complex. Relying on the location of the planets within the twelve houses of a subject's chart, some astrologers claim that they can advise clients about business partnerships and help them decide whom to hire. A question about a partnership is analyzed by a business astrologer named Yaschpaule on the "Astrology, Hand Analysis, Management Science and Business Prospects" Web page:

The 7th House deals with business partnership. . . . Those natives (subjects) having malefics or naturally evil planets like Mars, and Saturn in the 7th House should not have a business partnership. Either the partner will let him down, the partnership will be broken or there will be a financial loss.[30]

Yaschpaule also places much value in the planets and houses when discussing personnel management:

The 6th House deals with personnel. It reveals the working conditions of employees, and labor disturbances. A successful Personnel Manager should have a strong, favorable 6th House. If malefic (evil planets) like Mars . . . are sitting in the 6th House, the Personnel Manager will have frequent trouble with employees.[31]

## "An Accident of Birth"

Whether or not such predictions are accurate is open to question. Few executives would admit to making decisions based solely on astrology, and there are no objective records from which to draw conclusions. Further, in the modern workplace, where many forms of discrimination are illegal, companies would be open to lawsuits from those who were not hired, or were fired, because of their astrological charts. This ethical issue is the subject of Bob Steiner's essay, "Astrology Is Bigotry":

When one person evaluates another for a job, jury selection, criminal guilt, membership in an association, or any of several other areas of life, based upon the color of the person's skin, the person's religion, or the color of the person's eyes, there is a storm of protest. "Bigotry! Racism!" are the cries. And yet, when one human being evaluates the worth of another based upon an accident of birth—the date of birth, it is accepted. It is called astrology. . . . [And] astrology is bigotry.[32]

## The Elements of Love

Such charges are dismissed by believers, who compare astrology to a road map that allows an individual to chart a course through the hazards of life. For some the most perilous journeys involve matters of the heart, and astrologers have long consulted the stars to help clients heal relationships or find true love. This is accomplished by comparing the astrological data of the subjects and analyzing the personal characteristics ostensibly revealed by birth charts. The reasoning behind this process is explained by Terry Lamb in *Born to Be Together*:

> We can come to better self-understanding by studying and working with our own chart. We can understand our partner better by coming to know their chart. We can learn about . . . our way of relating with each other by studying the way our charts connect with each other.[33]

The most immediate method for determining astrological compatibility is through the four elements: earth, air, fire, or water. These designations were first used in ancient civilizations by those who believed that the physical body was ruled by earth, emotions by water, and thoughts by air. The spark of life itself—the soul that animated a person to life—was believed to be ruled by fire. Through this philosophy, people who were solid and dependable were regarded as earthy; those who were sensitive and emotional were watery; thinkers and intellectuals were airy; brave and energetic people were fiery.

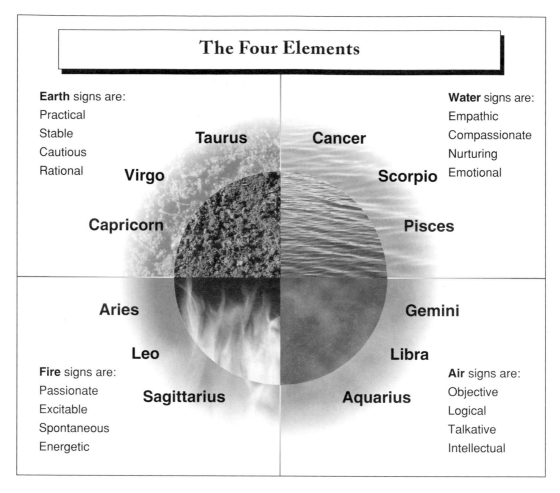

**The Four Elements**

**Earth** signs are:
Practical
Stable
Cautious
Rational

Taurus

Virgo

Capricorn

Cancer

Scorpio

Pisces

**Water** signs are:
Empathic
Compassionate
Nurturing
Emotional

Aries

Leo

Gemini

Libra

**Fire** signs are:
Passionate
Excitable
Spontaneous
Energetic

Sagittarius

Aquarius

**Air** signs are:
Objective
Logical
Talkative
Intellectual

*Each of the four elements—Earth, Water, Air, and Fire—is associated with three sun signs, as shown in this chart.*

The ancient Greeks applied the four elements to the personal characteristics associated with each sun sign. Therefore, Taurus, Virgo, and Capricorn are classified as earth signs who are practical, stable, cautious, and rational. Gemini, Libra, and Aquarius are air signs and have thoughtful airy qualities that make a person objective, logical, and talkative. According to Lamb, air people also "love to flit around, exploring a variety of interests, getting to know a wide range of people."[34]

Aries, Leo, and Sagittarius are fire signs who are said to be passionate, excitable, and spontaneous. Cancer, Scorpio, and Pisces purportedly possess traits of the water element, making them empathic, compassionate, and nurturing.

Using such classifications, people are said to get along best with those who share a similar element. Hence, two people who were born under earth signs are said to be in harmony with one another. Elements that complement each other are also said to be harmonious. Therefore, a relationship between a fire person and an air person would be favorable because fire needs air to burn. Fire, however, would not do well with earth or water, according to Lamb, because fire "might feel 'put out' by water's sensitivity and smothered by earth's heaviness."[35]

## Negative Characteristics

The analogies of the elements may be limited, though. For example, most astrologers say that water is compatible with earth, but according to "Marilyn's Astrology" Web page, "Water and Earth . . . make mud."[36] Elements also have negative characteristics that are ignored by astrologers who often try to accentuate the positive. For example, earth people can purportedly be materialistic and suspicious, while air people can be overly analytical, detached, or impractical. However, one school of thought uses such negative personal characteristics as a way of counseling the lovelorn. For example, in *How to Spot a Bastard by His Sun Sign*, Adele Lang and Susi Rajah harshly characterize fire-sign men as "Out-of-control control freaks. Untalented show-offs . . . [and] self-proclaimed demi-gods."[37] Presumably, these would be people to avoid.

Analyzing personalities by the four elements is only the most general form of relationship astrology. The sun signs are equally important, as are the planets and their aspects. When the charts of two people are involved, there are hundreds of recommendations that an astrologer can make concerning a couple.

## Medical Astrology

People in bad love relationships often call on astrologers to help them mend a symbolic broken heart. Others use astrology to determine whether or not they might be suffering from real heart conditions or other medical problems. According to Goodman: "Your individual birth chart indicated at the moment of your first breath of life on this Earth the weak links in your body's chain reactions."[38]

These weak links are used by medical astrologers to counsel clients in ways to live healthier lives. For example, because they are ruled by the sun, Leos are said to have a predisposition to heart problems, the heart being the center of the body as the sun is the center of the solar system. Recognizing this, an astrologer can warn a Leo to reduce fats in the diet, exercise more often, and keep a watchful eye on levels of bad cholesterol, an indicator of future heart disease. A skeptic might point out that this advice would be applicable to anybody, no matter when they were born. Yet astrology has been associated with health and well-being since at least A.D. 10, when the Roman poet Manilius wrote the book *Astronomicon*, which linked each sign to specific parts of the body. Since that time, astrologers have believed that Gemini rules the arms, shoulders, fingers, lungs, and upper ribs; Virgo the large and small intestine and pancreas; and Scorpio the nose, genitals, blood, and back. This school of thought dictates that if a sign rules a specific body part, then that bone, organ, appendage, or fluid can be susceptible to problems. Goodman claims that such knowledge is useful for preventing problems:

> [Your] horoscope shows which diseases and accidents to which parts of your personal body you are *inclined* to suffer. If you take the proper preventative measures, your astrological birth warnings will have accomplished their purpose, and you need *not* become ill in the manner indicated in the horoscope. . . .

# Suicides and Astrology

When a person has suicidal tendencies, it would seem reasonable that such personal traits would be strongly indicated in his or her birth chart. However, as H.J. Eysenck and D.K.B. Nias write in *Astrology: Science or Superstition?*, one comprehensive test could find no such link:

> If our characters or destinies are written in the stars, then surely a tendency to suicide is one thing that ought to show up in our birth charts. Also, suicides generally occur at a known time, they are recorded and they must be certified by law. . . . For these reasons, suicide forms a particularly good field for astrological research, and it has been the subject of an excellent study by Nona Press and others. Press and her colleagues looked at the records of suicides in New York City from 1969 to 1973, selecting those who had been born in the city and whose birth certificates showed the times of birth. They ended up with 311 suitable candidates, and matched each suicide with a control born in the same year and borough and chosen from birth certificates sampled by random numbers. . . .
>
> A large number of astrological factors were then entered into a computer, and each factor was tested for significance between suicides and controls in each of the three groups. Altogether about 100,000 different factors were examined in each of the 622 charts. . . . Of all the 100,000 factors examined, none correlated significantly with suicide in a way that was reproduced over the three groups. Out of all the possible astrological influences in the birth chart, this huge and very thorough study failed to find a single one that was significantly related to suicide.

But if you do *not* take such preventative measure . . . then your body will be inclined to respond to the electromagnetic pulls [of the planets] and what were originally only possibilities will then become realities.[39]

Whatever the accuracy of Goodman's statement, there has been a move since the 1970s to use astrology not only as a predictor of health problems but also as a way of healing a patient. This concept is tied in with another ancient belief, that each plant and herb has its own constellation and planet and can be used in conjunction with astrology to cure disease. For example, herbs such as borage and hawthorn berries are said to fall under the sign of Leo because they are believed to strengthen the heart, lower blood pressure, and improve circulation. Because Gemini is associated with the lungs, plants under that sign, such as coltsfoot, are used to cure bronchitis, asthma, and whooping cough.

## Astrology in the Maternity Ward

There is little scientific evidence linking astrology to the medicinal qualities of herbs. However, there have been several studies conducted to ascertain if astrological conditions can influence a person's health.

In 1977, medical researcher Larry Michelson attempted to link astrology with a medical condition in babies known as respiratory distress syndrome, or RDS. This unpredictable condition, which affects the lungs, can kill a baby unexpectedly within three hours of birth, often before doctors can detect that anything is wrong. Searching for an astrological link, Michelson compared the birth charts of 122 babies known to have had RDS with those of 24,000 healthy babies. Taking into account many technical statistical variables, Michelson discovered that RDS babies were most likely to be Aquarians and that there were ten other strong astrological indicators that predicted RDS. For example, RDS babies were more likely than average to be born when Jupiter was sextile (at a sixty degree angle) to Neptune, the sun was squared with Neptune, or when Sagittarius was rising.

By applying this information to babies about to born, Michelson was able to correctly predict RDS 69 percent of the time. If such analysis were consistently possible, it could be used to save the lives of thousands of infants every year. Other researchers, however, could not replicate Michelson's study. Independent statisticians found errors because the number of babies tested was too small.

Another study, which began in a London children's hospital in 1958 and continued for more than four decades, has been used by some who have tried to debunk astrological belief. This investigation tracked two thousand people who were called time twins because they were born within minutes of each other in early March of that year. The research was originally conducted to determine how birth circumstances can affect future health, but was correlated to personality characteristics by Geoffrey Dean, a scientist and former astrologer in Perth, Australia, and Ivan Kelly, a psychologist at the University of Saskatchewan, Canada. The researchers tabulated more than a hundred different characteristics from the subjects, including occupation, marital status, aggressiveness, IQ levels, and abilities in art, sports, and mathematics. While astrologers have long claimed that these characteristics are determined by the positions of the stars and planets, the study showed that the time twins were not similar in any ways that might be expected.

*Some astrologers claim that they can predict whether babies will develop respiratory distress syndrome, a life-threatening condition.*

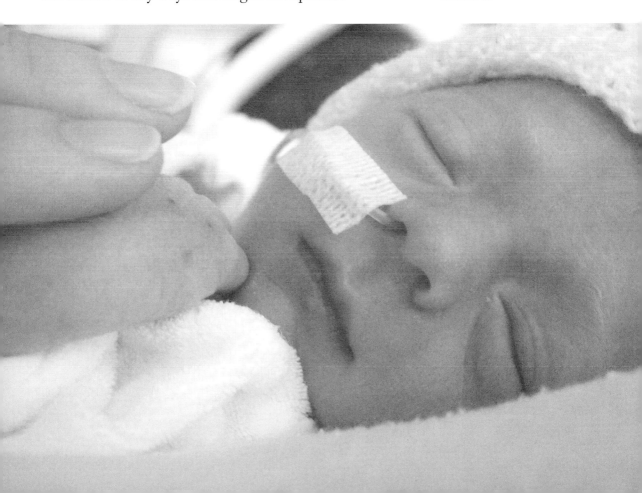

In an August 2003 *Times of India* article, "Astrology is Rubbish, Says New Research," Dean says the consistency of the findings weighs heavily against astrology. "It has no acceptable mechanism, its principles are invalid and it has failed hundreds of tests. But no hint of these problems will be found in astrology books which, in effect, are exercises in deception." Dean adds that, as a former astrologer himself, he has become a target of scorn for believers. "I'm probably the most hated person in astrology because I'm regarded as a turncoat."[40]

Dean's study may satisfy the skeptics, but astrologers point out that natal charts are based on exacting birth statistics not studied by the researchers, including rising signs, planetary aspects, and other data that changes from one minute to the next. However, even this assertion has not satisfied nonbelievers, as Andrew Fraknoi writes:

> Astrologers seem to disagree on the most fundamental issues of their craft . . . most importantly—which personality traits go with which cosmic phenomena. Read ten different astrology columns, or have a reading done by ten different astrologers, and you will probably get ten different interpretations. If astrology is a science, as its proponents claim, why are its practitioners not converging on a consensus theory after thousands of years of gathering data and refining its interpretation? Scientific ideas generally converge over time as they are tested against laboratory or other evidence.[41]

Fraknoi's rhetorical questions will no doubt remain unanswered as long as astrologers produce horoscopes. Until the number of research studies can match the widespread dissemination of astrological findings, the mystery of personality determination will likely remain unsolved.

# Chapter 3

# Astrology's Influence on Daily Events

Most people encounter astrologers only when they read their horoscopes in the daily newspaper. Often published on the same page as the comics and a crossword puzzle, these one- or two-sentence forecasts are rarely taken seriously and are often extremely vague. For example, Libras reading the *Los Angeles Times* on October 20, 2005, are informed by astrologer Holly Mathis: "Part of your charm is that you believe in fairy tales."[42] These words may bring a smile to Libras, and might also explain the disclaimer at the end of the column: "The forecast should be read for entertainment [only]."[43]

For those who hope to get more depth from a daily forecast, it becomes necessary to study the movements, or transits, of the planets at any given moment. These transits can then be compared to the fixed positions of the planets on a person's birth chart. The relationships of the transiting planets to fixed planets are said to influence a person's day.

An analysis of transits can be very complicated. For example, if a person is born with Mercury, the planet symbolizing communication, at ten degrees Capricorn, according to Sakoian and Acker, he or she would be "capable of extended concentration and good organization."[44] However, that subject might have a difficult day if Neptune, a planet associated with delusional thoughts and fuzzy thinking, were transiting Capricorn. Neptune would also affect the subject's ability to make important decisions. An astrologer making a note of this would also observe the house through which Neptune was transiting and analyze its aspects to the other fixed planets in the birth chart.

*Horoscopes that appear in newspapers are viewed even by astrologers as little more than entertainment.*

*The sun is a powerful force in astrology, though the planets can also strongly influence events on Earth.*

## Planetary Pull and Interdependence

As is typical in astrology, this complex method of determining daily events gives the astrologer quite a bit of leeway when it comes to exact details. The meanings of transits can be vague, contradictory, or unfathomable. Despite this shortcoming, astrologers have long been consulted to determine if a particular day is auspicious for planting crops, getting married, traveling, or even waging a battle or seeking peace. When asked how the movements of distant planets can affect an individual millions of miles away, some say that the heavenly bodies exert a gravitational force on all human beings. This is explained on the Web site astrology.com:

> In some ways, the forces between the Planets involved in Astrology can be simplified into one word: gravity. The Sun has the greatest gravity and the strongest effect in Astrology, followed by the Moon, the Earth's satellite. The other Planets are not truly satellites of the Earth, but nevertheless, they have gravity and so affect the Earth. The Sun controls the Earth's motion and the Moon controls its tides, but the other Planets have their own effects on the Earth—and on the people who live on Earth. Sometimes their influences can be so strong that they outweigh the Sun's energy![45]

There is little evidence to back such claims, however. Astronomers point out that the gravitational effect of the moon is fifty times more powerful than the rest of the planets combined, which should technically make the moon fifty times more important in a horoscope. In addition, the gravitational force of Mars is fifty times stronger when it is on the earth side of the sun than when it is on the opposite side. As astronomer Philip Plait writes: "Mars' gravitational influence on the Earth drops by a factor of more than 50 from one side of the Sun to the other. One would think this would be an incredibly important detail, yet it is ignored in most horoscopes."[46]

In the early days of astrological prediction, there was no such debate. Ancient astrologers did not understand

# Astrologer Joan Quigley's Science

Joan Quigley, who advised President Ronald Reagan and his wife, Nancy, during the 1980s, believes that her astrological method is based on science. On the Web page, "So Speaks the Soothsayer," D. Trull explains:

Quigley spends a good deal of time defending her brand of astrology as a valid and misunderstood "science," distinct from the tawdry newspaper horoscopes most people are familiar with.

"I base my astrological analysis on the data provided to me by astronomers and charts calculated by computers," she explains. "My conclusions are based on this accurate scientific material in the same way your doctor supports his diagnosis by the laboratory reports or an economist bases his predictions on statistics."

Quigley dismisses newspaper "Sun Sign" columns as "harmless and amusing," but not true astrology. "A person must be very credulous indeed to believe that the same thing is happening to one twelfth of the world's population during a given day or month," she wisely points out.

What makes Quigley's system of astrology different? Well, it constructs a horoscope for each person based on the exact moment of birth, preferably down to the precise minute. She explains that this information provides a chart that is genuinely accurate for every individual.

the distance of the planets from earth or even that they orbited the sun. Instead, they simply interpreted the planetary transits as movements of the gods and took comfort in knowing that their daily readings were of a divine nature. These forecasts were extremely important and, as long ago as 3800 B.C., Assyrian soothsayers were making daily astrological reports to kings who wished to be informed of all planetary occurrences in the heavens.

By 500 B.C. Egyptian pharaohs had taken the concept of daily horoscopes even further, requiring hourly reports. Soothsayers indicated that because of planetary positions, some hours were lucky, while others were ill-fated or ominous. The reasoning of the ancient astrologers is explained by Ellen McCaffery in *Astrology: Its History and Influence in the Western World*:

> The Egyptians believed in the mutual interdependence of all things in the universe and because of this they also believed in the inter-relationship between what was going on in the heavens and what was going on in the earth, going on in nature as a whole, and in human bodies and human affairs.[47]

The beliefs of the ancient Egyptians are echoed in the words of modern astrologers. In *The Case for Astrology*, John Anthony West and Jan Gerhard Toonder write, "Astrology is based upon the fundamental premise that celestial phenomena affect life and events on earth."[48]

## The President's Astrologer

Just as kings of old relied upon the prognostications of soothsayers, the rich and famous in recent times have also used astrologers to plot their daily lives. This was demonstrated in the late 1980s when it was learned that during his two terms as president, Ronald Reagan relied on the advice of San Francisco astrologer Joan Quigley.

Reagan and his wife, Nancy, had a long history of involvement with astrologers. Both were movie stars in 1950s Hollywood, where they often attended glamorous "zodiac parties" with celebrity astrologer Carroll Righter. In 1966, Nancy consulted with astrologers and psychics when Reagan successfully ran for governor of California. She first contacted Quigley in 1976 during her husband's failed bid for the presidency.

In 1980, Reagan won the Republican nomination for president, and Nancy once again consulted with Quigley. The astrologer studied Reagan's birth chart and made suggestions concerning the timing of campaign stops, public meetings, and speeches. Notably, Quigley was instrumental in picking the day of October 28 for Reagan's second debate with incumbent Jimmy Carter, since the astrologer believed that the planets were extremely unfavorable for the Libra Carter on that day. The debate was delayed to take advantage of this situation despite objections from Reagan's advisors, who were afraid that the event was too close to election day on November 4.

Reagan was widely judged to have won the debate and he handily won the election a few days later against what some observers considered to be long odds. Whether or not the president's success was determined by the stars remains unknown.

## Planning the President's Schedule

Reagan had been president only a few months when, on March 30, 1981, a troubled young man named John Hinckley Jr. shot and nearly killed him. Although Reagan survived, the First Lady was terrified that another assassination attempt might succeed. Once again, Nancy called Quigley, who studied the positions of the planets in relation to Reagan's birth chart. The astrologer determined that March 30 was a dangerous day for the president to have been traveling and speaking in public and she would have advised against it. At this time, the First Lady hired Quigley to study the president's astrological transits and aspects every day. She also had special phone lines installed in the White House and the presidential retreat at Camp David for consultations with Quigley.

In the following years, during many long conversations with the First Lady, Quigley helped plan the president's schedule. Her instructions were turned over to Reagan's advisor and deputy chief-of-staff, Michael Deaver, who carried them out.

According to Quigley, as Reagan's personal astrologer, she chose the exact time of departure for the president's trips, the best day and hour for congressional meetings, and the timing and location of important international conferences.

*After President Ronald Reagan was nearly assassinated on March 30, 1981, astrologer Joan Quigley told Nancy Reagan that she could have predicted that the day held danger for the president.*

*President Ronald Reagan and First Lady Nancy Reagan sought the advice of San Francisco astrologer Joan Quigley.*

When Reagan met with Soviet leader Mikhail Gorbachev to discuss nuclear weapons reductions, the president was purportedly armed with suggestions from his astrologer for demands that should be made during the negotiations. Quigley later stated that her work helped Reagan win two presidential elections, protected him from several potential assassins, and helped make his diplomatic meetings with Gorbachev a success.

During Reagan's second term, Deaver was replaced by Donald Regan, who was not happy taking instructions from Quigley. This caused friction with the First Lady, who allegedly insisted the president fire the chief-of-staff. In 1988, Regan wrote a memoir that revealed the president's reliance on an astrologer. The revelation caused a sensation in the media and generated much criticism of the president and his wife. Later the First Lady wrote her own memoir, *My Turn*, in which she explained her rationale for hiring Quigley:

> While I was never certain that Joan's astrological advice was helping to protect Ronnie, the fact is that nothing like March 30 ever happened again. . . . Was astrology one of those reasons? I don't really believe it was, but I don't really believe it wasn't. But I know this: It didn't hurt, and I'm not sorry I did it.[49]

## Business Soothsayers

Nancy Reagan's rationale for hiring Quigley was that the astrologer's advice would reduce risk to the president. Risk is also a factor for those who wish to succeed in business, and there is a growing subculture of executives who attribute their success to business astrologers. For example, Seattle businessman Michael Anderson was searching for the best day to incorporate his online training company, Avant Institute, in 2003. Anderson believed the business would be profitable if it had a propitious "birthday." Anderson contacted Madeline Gerwick-Brodeur, a business astrologer who helps companies and executives figure out the best timing for business planning, marketing, and relocation. Gerwick-Brodeur created a horoscope linking the position of the planets to Anderson's business activities and goals. By noting these planetary cycles, she found the specific day that would be most promising for Anderson's business. While there is no proven connection between Gerwick-Brodeur's advice and Avant's accomplishments, in less than a year, the company reached $400,000 in sales.

## A Growing Field

The field of business astrology has grown in recent years, and those wishing to enter it can study for bachelor's and master's degrees in astrological studies at Kepler College in Washington State. However, faculty member Georgia Stathis told *San Francisco Chronicle* reporter Julie N. Lynem that astrology is still not accepted as a method of business planning: "We are still in a day and age where if you tell the public or your stockholders or whomever that you are using astrology, it isn't the same as using an economist or any other sort of analyst to help your business."[50]

Critics of astrology point out that human effort and economic factors, not planetary transits, have the greatest effects on a business. Further, many nonbelievers ask the age-old question: If astrologers are as good as they claim, why do they themselves not make millions in business?

Some astrologers answer that the planets indicate only general trends, not specific information about a particular situation. Astrologer Jack Fertig supplies another answer:

> Many of us began the study of astrology as a spiritual pursuit rather than a commercial one. The field is predominant with people who consider philosophical and spiritual wealth far more important than money. Still, most of us are indeed richer than we

*An astrologer in Thailand gives advice to a client. The practice of consulting astrologers before making business decisions is growing.*

would be without astrology, both financially and philosophically. There are many branches of astrology and very few astrologers use astrology for financial investments—usually because skills and interests lie in other fields. Some astrologers can see that they have no chart for making money, but may help those who do.[51]

## The Influences of the Great Ages

Business astrology tends to focus on the individual and the planetary influence on a particular day. However, one school of astrological thought looks at the big picture and studies the ways that the major constellations, not the planets, influence daily events on earth. In this view, each sign holds sway for approximately two thousand years, and the influences change with the precession of the equinoxes.

When an early civilization was founded in Mesopotamia around 4300 B.C., the constellation Taurus was on the horizon on the first day of spring. Hence, this era is known as the Age of Taurus. Ruled by the goddess Venus, the period was one in which agriculture, associated with feminine qualities, first developed. In addition, the Great Pyramids were built in Egypt, while sacred circles such as Stonehenge were built in Europe.

Astrologers say such monuments are reflective of the Taurean talent for building and architecture. The influence of Taurus is also said to have inspired people in Assyria, Egypt, and Crete to deify the bull and dedicate religious cults to this animal. As gods incarnate, individual bulls were worshipped in temples, stabled in majestic quarters, fed the best foods, and given herds of the finest cows.

Astrologers believe that the influence of Taurus on daily life was also seen in India, where Hinduism developed during the Taurean age. According to the *Rig Veda*, or Hindu scriptures written during that time:

Cows are the foremost of all things. Themselves sacred, they are the best of cleansers and sanctifiers. People should cherish cows for obtaining prosperity and even peace. Cows are said to represent the highest energy both in this world and the world that is above. There is nothing that is more sacred or sanctifying than cows.[52]

## The Arrival of the Ram

The Age of Taurus passed into the Age of Aries around 2400 B.C. As the new age dawned, people found it necessary to symbolically kill Taurus, according to Maria K. Simms in *Millennium: Fears, Fantasies & Facts: Astrologists Predict 2000*:

> The ancients decided that a whole new order had arrived. The constellation that now rose right with the sun, and was thus invisible, was said to be "sacrificed." At the dawn of the Age of Aries, one of the most popular animals to be offered on the sacrificial altars was the bull or calf, a symbol of the "sacrificed" Age of Taurus. The symbol of the Age of Aries was the Ram, and ram or fire deities quickly began to compete with the bull-gods and sacred cows for the devotion of the people. As the new order became more firmly established, those who slipped back into the old ways worshipped a watered-down version of the bull, a little bull—the golden calf.[53]

Since Mars, the god of war, rules Aries, daily life in the new age was purportedly dominated by aggressive male energy, violence, wars, and conquest. During this period of nearly twenty centuries, empires in Persia, Greece, and Rome expanded and conquered foreign lands. In some regions, such as Assyria and Greece, warrior societies

developed, massive armies were formed, and thousands of warships were launched to wage battle.

The Age of Aries also saw the kingdom of Israel established in Palestine by followers of Judaism. Since that time, when Jews celebrate the new year, they blow on a ram's horn, called a shofar, as a call to repentance. The Jewish religion was also among the first to worship a single male god as opposed to the multitude of gods and goddesses revered by other religious cultures. Astrologers believe that this powerful monotheistic male energy at the base of the dominant religion was influenced by the Age of Aries.

*Some astrologers say that the dominance of Taurus (shown here) between 4300 B.C. and 2400 B.C. explains the construction of monuments like the Egyptian pyramids.*

## The Piscean Age

Around 200 B.C. the Age of Pisces was ushered in as the constellation Aries failed to appear at dawn on the first day of spring. While skeptics point out that war and aggressive male energy have remained constant throughout human history, believers of the great astrological ages contend that people's day-to-day lives were changed by the arrival of Pisces.

FEBRUARI

The constellation of Pisces resembles two fish pointing in opposite directions. Because Pisces is traditionally ruled by Jupiter, the supreme god of Rome, the sign is often associated with major religions. For this reason, the Age of Pisces is said to be dominated by Judaism, Islam, Buddhism, and especially Christianity, as the birth of Jesus coincides with the dawning of the Age of Pisces. According to Simms: "By the end of the Age of Aries, the ram had become a lamb; and as Aries became lost, or sacrificed, in the sunrise as the Age of Pisces dawned, Christ was understood to be the sacrificial lamb—the Lamb of God who gave his own life for the redemption of humanity."[54]

Such beliefs remain controversial, and some feel that astrology is an occult practice that should be wholly disassociated from religion. Despite these objections, however, astrologers contend that miracles such as Jesus walking on water or feeding five thousand people with only two fish are part of the Piscean dominance over human affairs. "The Transition of Ages—Pisces to Aquarius" Web page elaborates on this:

> Christ did his work utilizing the energy of Pisces, the sign of the [twin] Fishes. . . . These forces impacted our world . . . during the Age of Pisces, and the truth of our essential duality—body and soul—was revealed. The sign itself shows the linking of the two fishes, as our soul and body are linked. The evolutionary work of this age has been the lifting of our lower physical nature to that of the soul. Christ, in the age, has shown the way—the fusion or blending of soul and form to produce the incarnate Christ in all.[55]

Around A.D. 1300, the second fish of Pisces came into view. Since this fish faces the opposite direction, its influence is said to have been contradictory to the deeply religious aspects of the earlier age. Astrologers believe that this second

*Opposite Page:*
*In this postcard created in the 1920s, the artist depicts the astrological sign for Pisces.*

fish gave rise to the growth of intellectualism and art that marked the Renaissance in the fifteenth century and the Age of Enlightenment that followed. During these eras, intellectuals celebrated human reason rather than blind faith, promoted science over superstition, and visualized governments free from tyrannical leaders. According to astrologer E. Alan Meece, "This . . . age was one of science, intellectual analysis . . . rational thought and the growing power of the secular state and bureaucracy."[56]

## The Dawning of the Age of Aquarius

Pisces is still said to influence life today, but the constellation is slowly passing, and astrologers call the present time the dawning of the Age of Aquarius. Dawning is a relative term, however, as the constellation Aquarius is not expected

# The Age of Aquarius

The Rosicrucian Fellowship, as explained on "The Aquarian Age" Web page, is an ancient Christian sect that believes in the "Christian Mystic Philosophy . . . [that will] help prepare mankind for the coming age of Universal Brotherhood, the Age of Aquarius." The Web page offers further Rosicrucian details about the Age of Aquarius:

The Aquarian Age will bring with it an era of universal brotherhood, in preparation for which we see the barriers of race prejudice being broken all around us. To be sure, this is presently being accomplished under conditions of bloodshed and revolt. We can be certain, however, that although the sword, which had its reign during the Piscean Age, still is powerful, SCIENCE and ALTRUISM [selflessness] will rule during the Aquarian Age.

Since Aquarius is an airy, scientific, and intellectual sign, it is a foregone conclusion that the religion of that Age must be rooted in reason and able to solve the riddle of life and death in a manner that will satisfy both the mind and the religious instinct. . . . When this point in evolution is reached, mankind also will be so much more enlightened that it will avoid many of the pitfalls which cause trouble today, and we will enjoy a much happier existence than has been the rule up to the present stage. We will be able to solve social problems in a manner equitable to all, and the use of improving machinery will free mankind from physical toil to a great extent and give him greater opportunity for intellectual and spiritual improvement.

to be visible on March 21 until the year 2600. Despite this fact, some believe that because the ages change so slowly, it can take centuries before a major shift in human behavior and consciousness occurs. Therefore, astrologers say, the power of Aquarius is already changing life on earth. As Simms explains: "The end of the old order overlaps with the new. By the time the constellation Aquarius rises with the Sun at the vernal equinox the vision of the new order will be firmly established."[57]

The symbol of Aquarius is the water bearer, whose flowing waters symbolize freedom, discovery, and the breaking of boundaries. These symbols were embraced by the those in the counterculture movement in the 1960s, when attitudes concerning authority, religion, government, marriage, and traditional values were undergoing rapid change. In 1968, the hit song "Aquarius," from the musical *Hair*, popularized the notion that the Age of Aquarius was dawning and would usher in a new age of harmony, under-standing, universal brotherhood, and the liberation of the mind from falsehoods and violent thoughts. Meece elabo-rates, writing that the Age of Aquarius will be "an age of knowledge, independent thought and demands for freedom and progress. The role of the individual and the organiza-tion will be coordinated into a humanitarian whole. Reli-gion and spirituality will be based on knowledge and experience instead of belief."[58]

It is said that Aquarius has already exerted its influence through the growth of the Aquarian Age movement, now called the New Age movement. The movement spurred widespread interest in Eastern religion and formerly eso-teric spiritual practices such as channeling, crystal healing, fortune-telling, and meditation.

Astrology played a strong role in bringing the New Age movement to a much wider audience in August 1987, when there was a historic alignment of Mercury, Venus, Mars, and the Sun. This event, called the Harmonic Convergence, culminated on August 24, when the new moon transited through the aligned planets. During the preceding week, groups of New Age spiritualists gathered to celebrate a new era at spiritual sites throughout the world, such as Stonehenge in England and Sedona in Arizona. Described in terms similar to those used for the Age of Aquarius, the Harmonic Convergence was supposed to bring a global awakening of love, peace, unity, and universal cooperation. While the event was largely dismissed by the mainstream, some in the New Age movement believe the planetary alignment was responsible for influencing major geopolitical events, especially the collapse of repressive Communist governments in the Soviet Union and Eastern Europe in the late 1980s.

## Plutonian Transformation of the United States

Most analysts say communism fell because it was based on an inefficient system that could not globally compete with the United States. And there has certainly been no shortage of war and violence since the Harmonic Convergence. However, astrologers say that the positive effects of the Harmonic Convergence, like the Aquarian influences, might not be realized for decades or even centuries. In addition, astrological influences are ever changing. The positive astrological influences on life one day might turn negative and harmful the next as the relationship of the planets to the earth changes. And sometimes positive aspects might have negative consequences, according to psychologist and astrologer Liz Greene.

Greene has done an extensive analysis of the astrological influences in place during the terrorist attacks on the United States on September 11, 2001. When the astrologer studied the positions of the stars and planets at 8:45 A.M., when the first jet hit the World Trade Center, she found that there was a powerful and harmonious configuration between the

planets Mercury, Saturn, Uranus, and Neptune. Generally, this would be read as an encouraging influence. However, according to Greene:

*A gathering of believers in astrology listens to a speaker at a celebration of the Harmonic Convergence.*

> This set-up of planets is telling us something we may not wish to recognize: it is easy for such [attacks] to occur when the collective psyche floats in a state of complacency and unawareness. Such planetary configurations are aspects of ease . . . but they can also connote a naive assumption that all is well in the world. . . . This planetary alignment is in the astrological element of air—concerned with ideas, ideals, and concepts—and perhaps reflects the dangerously self-satisfied idealism with which we in the Western world began the week of 9th September.[59]

Greene cautions that it would have been impossible to have predicted the terrorist event; the influences spelled out by the configurations are not that obvious.

# Astrological Influences on 9/11

*Some astrologers say that planetary influences help pave the way for the terrorist attacks of September 11, 2001.*

Astrologers who have charted the planetary powers allegedly in place during the September 11, 2001, terrorist attacks in New York have found that Saturn and Pluto were in opposition to each other. Although *The Astrologer's Handbook* was written twenty-eight years before the attack on the World Trade Center, the aspects of the opposing planets, written by Frances Sakoian and Louis S. Acker, present an unsettling description of the planetary influences occurring during the event:

This opposition indicates serious karmic problems. The natives [subjects] can be the perpetrators or victims of oppression, cruelty, and harsh treatment, usually because of their personal connection with adverse conditions of mass destiny which thwart their ambitions and endanger their safety. Saturn, as the grim reaper, will bring misfortune into their lives. Individuals who are raised in slums, severely underprivileged, cruelly treated, or caught in wars, or who are unjustly imprisoned, are likely to have this opposition. . . . Sometimes the deaths of the natives are fated in some peculiar way.

However, by comparing the astrological chart of 9/11 with the birth chart of the United States, Greene analyzes how the terrorist attack continues to influence daily life in America.

Greene begins with the idea that the United States was born when the Declaration of Independence was signed at about 5:10 P.M., July 4, 1776, in Philadelphia. At that time, the sun was in Cancer, but more important, Sagittarius was in ascent. This reflects a key astrological influence, according to Greene, that "has always been evident to the outside world in attractive and less attractive ways—the undaunted explorer's spirit, the boundless enthusiasm and faith in the future . . . the material and emotional excess, the assumption of moral superiority, the courageous refusal to accept defeat, the unquenchable optimism."[60]

When the attack occurred, Pluto was in opposition to Saturn, which is considered to be an ill omen. In addition, Pluto was crossing the Sagittarius ascent, and Plutonian transits are often associated with death, aggression, conflict, and other negative traits. Greene explains:

> Pluto moving across this Sagittarius Ascendant is a kind of Childhood's End, bringing with it the loss of innocence and the challenge of transforming Sagittarius' childlike intuitive vision of higher purpose into genuine wisdom and a more realistic vision of humanity. Pluto can take us to hell and back, and its process can involve loss, humiliation, depression, and a sense of colliding with fate or forces beyond our control. Pluto transits are humbling and may also be accompanied by feelings of impotence and great anxiety. The terrorist attack on 11th September is the major trigger for Plutonian transformation.[61]

Greene's analysis offers astrological insight into a terrible tragedy, but even the astrologer admits that it is all too easy to interpret planetary influences after an event. Most analysts would attribute the World Trade Center attack to human evil, not planetary powers. Astrologers, however, believe that there is more at work than the malevolent machinations of the terrorists, and transiting orbits and astrological aspects should be factored into the equation. For those who believe, events both good and bad are not only matters of fact, but matters of faith in the power of the planets.

# Chapter 4

# Forecasting and Transforming the Future

In the sixteenth century, English philosopher and states-man Francis Bacon wrote that it was possible to use "ce-lestial indicators" to produce reliable predictions about the weather, plagues, crops, and coming instances of "seditions and schisms."[62] Like many before him, Bacon believed that astrologers could use their craft to help people in the present plan for the unknown future. Indeed, astrologers have always been consulted to forecast the outcome of endeavors concerning love, marriage, war, health, and wealth. Ad-dressing this ancient practice, R. Campbell Thompson writes in *The Reports of Magicians and Astrologers*:

> Nothing was too great or too small to become the subject of an astrological forecast, and every event, from a national calamity such as a famine or disaster to the army, down to the appearance of the humblest peasant's last born child, was seriously considered and proved to be the result of causes which had al-ready been duly recognized.[63]

The predictive methods used by ancient astrologers have changed little in thousands of years. When an astrologer wants to predict the future, or prognosticate, he or she will track the imminent positions and transits of the planets. The influences of these approaching configurations are linked to the natal charts of the subject in question. If the planets are moving into favorable positions, the person, organization, or nation will purportedly see good things in the immediate future. If the planets are opposed, squared, or exhibit other unfavorable aspects, a negative state of affairs may ensue.

## Planets and Progressions

Planetary influences can be determined by methods more complicated than transits. A technique called progression is based on the belief that the position of the planets on a person's first day of life predicts that person's first year. The location of planets on the second day predicts the second year, and so on.

By using progressions, an astrologer looking into the near future of a twenty-one-year-old woman would use the "day-for-a-year" formula to study the positions of the planets on that woman's twenty-second day of life. For example, if the subject was born on August 1, this would make her a fun-loving Leo. However, on the twenty-second day of the woman's life, the sun moved into Virgo.

*The sixteenth-century English philosopher and statesman Francis Bacon believed that astrologers could predict the future.*

Projecting this onto the subject's twenty-second year, an astrologer might say that at this time, the Virgo energy will make the woman more studious and hardworking. Similarly, the conditions of the woman's life when she turns forty can ostensibly be predicted by studying the planetary aspects on her fortieth day of life.

A complete astrological prediction would use both transits and progressions, producing a chart with three concentric circles. The natal chart is placed at the center and overlaid with a circle showing progressions. This second chart is said to reveal inner changes in personality and interests. For instance, a person whose sun is progressing into

*Some witches, such as this one, use planetary influences not just to predict the future, but to change it.*

Sagittarius will become more philosophical or religious and express an interest in foreign cultures or legal matters.

A third chart showing transits is placed over the others. This third circle predicts potential environments and external conditions. For example, a favorable transit of Jupiter in a person's chart is said to determine wealth or a chance for advancement, while Saturn transits are said to stir up conditions in the environment that are detrimental to prosperity. By analyzing the many aspects revealed in the three charts, the astrologer claims to forecast the future.

## Astrology and Magic

In addition to predicting coming events, astrology is used by some who believe they can use the powers of the planets to alter or transform the future. These people, often called witches and magicians, chant magic spells, called invocations, that consist of special sets of words that allegedly can manipulate approaching events. When combined with the purported powers of the planets, magical spells are used to attempt to create wealth; cause someone to fall in love; or even spread bad luck, sickness, and death.

Practitioners of planetary magic, or magick, cast spells according to the phases of the moon. Those trying to create positive influences in the future—spells concerning love, success, fertility, health improvement, or wealth creation—perform magic rituals when the moon is waxing, or growing bigger. Those who cast spells of a destructive nature—causing a love affair to end or causing conflict, bad luck, or sickness—perform rituals when the moon is waning, or getting smaller.

Planetary magicians also associate the astrological powers of the planets with days of the week. For example, Sunday is ruled by the sun, and rituals performed on this day are used to create peace and harmony; make new friends; bring riches, honor, and glory; and prevent war.

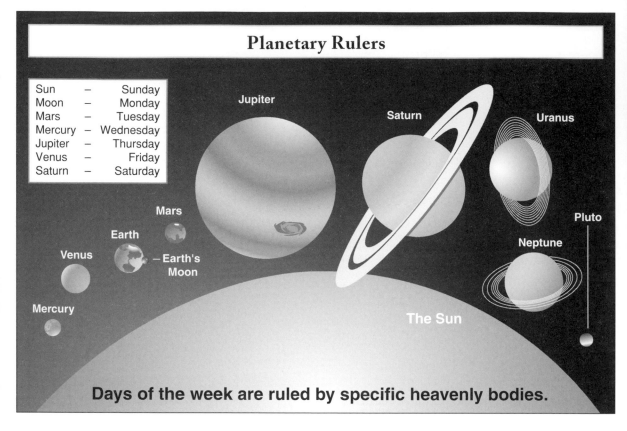

# Planetary Rulers

| | | |
|---|---|---|
| Sun | – | Sunday |
| Moon | – | Monday |
| Mars | – | Tuesday |
| Mercury | – | Wednesday |
| Jupiter | – | Thursday |
| Venus | – | Friday |
| Saturn | – | Saturday |

Jupiter

Saturn

Uranus

Mars

Earth

Pluto

Venus

—Earth's Moon

Neptune

Mercury

The Sun

**Days of the week are ruled by specific heavenly bodies.**

Monday is ruled by the moon, and moon magic is said to create safe voyages, influence a woman's fertility, and ensure good dreams in the coming days. Tuesday is ruled by the warrior Mars, and the energy of the red planet is used by those wishing to attain courage, achieve military success, or break negative spells. The power of Mars can also be used by practitioners of black magic to cause enemies to experience future strife, bitterness, and hardships.

Wednesday's planetary power is ruled by Mercury, whose energy is used to influence others and bring health and spiritual development. Thursday is associated with Jupiter. Spells cast on this day are meant to attract wealth, enhance male fertility, and bring luck to the workplace. Venus rules Friday and the force of this planet attracts love, happiness, new friendships, and luck in travel. Saturday is often associated with the negative energy of Saturn, so planetary magicians may cast spells on this day to ward off future evil, bring discord, or attack an enemy.

This method of using the planets to evoke, intensify, and direct the magic of spells is explained by Ray T. Marlbrough in *Charms, Spells & Formulas*:

> Let us suppose that you have just begun a new job and you want to [cast a spell] to build a good relationship with your boss. This would be considered constructive magick and would have a greater chance of success done during the waxing phase of the moon. Now we are going to look at the calendar . . . to see that the New Moon occurred five days ago. Therefore we are already in the correct phase of the moon and do not have to wait. Now we consult our table of influences for the days of the week. We see that the sun is associated with the gaining of favor from those in high places and it is also good for making friends. From this information we know that Sunday is good to begin this particular ritual. We therefore go back to our calendar to find out how many days we will have to wait until Sunday arrives during the waxing phase of the moon to begin our ritual.[64]

## Planetary Hours

Marlbrough's method for timing magical rituals is a basic system for using planetary magic. For thousands of years, astrologers have also associated planetary influences with each hour of the day. Under this system, the moon is said to rule the first hour of the week, which begins at sunrise on Monday. Each hour that follows, until midnight on Sunday, is ruled by a different heavenly body in the order of Saturn, Jupiter, Mars, Sun, Venus, and Mercury.

Ancient spell books, called grimoires, described the powers of each planetary hour. For example, the power of the Saturn hour is described in the grimoire *Key of Solomon*, published in the fifteenth century during the Renaissance:

> [In the] Hours of Saturn thou canst . . . operate to bring either good or bad fortune to buildings; to have familiar Spirits attend thee in sleep; to cause good or ill success to business, possessions, goods, seeds, fruits, and similar things, in order to acquire learning; to bring destruction and to give death, and to sow hatred and discord.[65]

Because various hours hold alleged powers, magicians can cast their spells at specific times to add strength to their magic. For example, a magician hoping to bring money into her life would recognize that the Jupiter hours, according to the *Key of Solomon*, "are proper for obtaining honors, acquiring riches . . . and arriving at all that thou canst desire."[66] Therefore, she would cast her spell on Thursday, also ruled by Jupiter. Using a chart listing the planetary hours, the magician would learn that the hours ruled by Jupiter on Thursday are the first, eighth, and fifteenth hours after sunrise. She could then pick one of those times to cast her spell to ostensibly attain money in her future.

## The Predictions of Nostradamus

The *Key of Solomon* was one of the magical texts published during the Renaissance. This book was likely used by soothsayer Michel de Nostredame, or Nostradamus, who used astrology and magical spells not to influence the future, but to forecast coming events.

Nostradamus was born in France in 1503 and was trained as a physician and astrologer. In 1555, he wrote a collection of prophecies called *Centuries*. In them, Nostradamus predicted world events through 3797, at which

time he said the world would end. The ten short books, which have never been out of print since they were first published, are today contained in one volume.

*Centuries* is so titled because the predictions are organized into nine groups of 100, except for one set of 42. These 942 prophecies consist of four-line poems called quatrains. Like thousands of astrologers before and since, Nostradamus deliberately made his predictions difficult to decipher. He wrote them in Latin, Greek, and Old French, a language that was antiquated even in the sixteenth century.

*Nostradamus works at his desk making complex astronomical calculations.*

In addition, he invented words and inserted anagrams—words formed by reordering the letters of another word or phrase.

Despite their deliberately evasive language, the prophecies of Nostradamus have been connected to dozens of historical events that have taken place in the last four and a half centuries. Believers say the astrologer predicted, among other things, the Great London Fire in 1666 and the French Revolution in the late eighteenth century. He was also said to have predicted the invention of the submarine, which he called an "iron fish," and the rocket, described as a "contraption of flying fire."[67]

# Garbled Words

*Those who believe in the predictions of Nostradamus (pictured) have been accused of deliberately distorting or misquoting his writings.*

After the terrorist attacks on the World Trade Center on September 11, 2001, it was said that Nostradamus predicted the tragic event. However, in the hours and days after the terrorist attacks, the soothsayer's words were deliberately misquoted by those wishing to make the case. The following six-line poem, which appeared on the Urban Legends and Folklore Web site, is a distortion of the "new city" quatrain:

Two steel birds will fall from the sky on the Metropolis. The sky will burn at forty-five degrees latitude. Fire approaches the great new city. Immediately a huge, scattered flame leaps up. Within months, rivers will flow with blood. The undead will roam earth for little time.

This example is just one of many in which people have garbled the words of an already ambiguous astrologer in order to claim that Nostradamus accurately foresaw various tragedies in modern times.

## Did Nostradamus Predict 9/11?

Nostradamus has also been credited with predicting events in the United States, a country that did not even exist in the sixteenth century. Such events include the destruction of the twin towers of the World Trade Center by hijackers on September 11, 2001. To back this claim, believers single out the verses from Century Six, quatrains ninety-seven and ninety-eight, as pertaining to the event:

> At forty-five degrees the sky will burn, Fire to approach the great new city: In an instant a great scattered flame will leap up, When one will want to demand proof from the Normans. Ruin . . . so very terrible with fear, Their great city stained, pestilential dead: To plunder the Sun and Moon and to violate their temples: And to redden the two rivers flowing with blood.[68]

Believers say that New York City lies "near" forty-five degrees, at forty degrees latitude north, and that the "two rivers" could be the Hudson and East rivers that flow around Manhattan. Skeptics point out, however, that New York is three hundred miles south of forty-five degrees. They say Nostradamus was really writing about Villeneuve-sur-Lot in France, as the word Villeneuve means "new city" and the town actually is located at forty-five degrees latitude. Moreover, the Normans are descendents of tenth-century Scandinavians who later ruled England. Their inclusion in this quatrain would have little to do with events on 9/11.

Those who believe in the accuracy of Nostradamus's predictions say that his writings foretold of a series of tyrannical leaders called anti-Christs. Some say that one of those anti-Christs was German dictator Adolf Hitler, whose invasion of Poland in 1939 triggered World War II. The relevant lines describe "a man stained with murder . . . the great enemy of the human race . . . one who was worse than any who had gone before." Later the quatrain reads:

He shall come to tyrannize the land. He shall raise up a hatred that had long been dormant. The child of Germany observes no law. Cries, and tears, fire, blood, and battle. A captain of Germany shall come to yield himself by false hope, So that his revolt shall cause great bloodshed.

*Some who believe in Nostradamus's predictions claim that he foretold the rise of Nazi leader Adolf Hitler (pictured).*

In the following stanza, some experts say that Nostradamus actually referred to Hitler by name but missed by one letter:

Beasts wild with hunger will cross the rivers The greater part of the battlefield will be against Hister.[69]

## Hitler's Astrologers

Whether or not Nostradamus was actually referring to Adolf Hitler, several high-ranking Nazis were known to consult with astrologers for political and military advice; in the late 1930s, Hitler himself received an astonishingly accurate prediction from astrologer Karl Ernst Krafft.

Krafft was an ardent supporter of the Nazis and often studied Hitler's astrological chart, plotting the dictator's planetary transits and progressions. In late October 1939, Krafft divined that Hitler would face an assassination attempt by someone using an explosive device. The astrologer immediately passed this information to a member of the German intelligence service, who disregarded the prognostication. On November 9, when a bomb exploded in a Munich beer hall moments after Hitler left, Krafft sent a telegram to a

Nazi official reminding him that he predicted the event. The letter was passed to Propaganda Minister Joseph Goebbels, who had the astrologer arrested and questioned about his role in the assassination attempt. After Krafft convinced Goebbels that his predictions were accurate, the propaganda minister hired him to work for the Nazis. However, the astrologer soon fell out of favor with Goebbels, who sent Krafft to a concentration camp, where he died in 1944.

Despite the fate of Krafft, several Nazi officials continued to seek advice about the future from astrologers. When the Nazis faced near-certain defeat in January 1944, Walter Schellenberg, the officer in charge of counterespionage, considered a plan to overthrow Hitler and save Germany. In order to determine the outcome of this plan, the officer asked astrologer Wilhelm Wulff to study the progressions and transits of Soviet leader Joseph Stalin and the birth charts of the Soviet Union, Great Britain, and the United States. Wulff informed Schellenberg that Stalin and the Soviet Union had a large number of favorable planetary transits coming in 1945 and 1946. Writing in his autobiography, *Zodiac and Swastika*, Wulff also said he pointed out that the prospects of the United States and Great Britain were, "Much the same as the Soviet Union's! To put it bluntly, the constellations of these two nations are extremely advantageous right up to 1947. They reach a peak in mid-May 1945.

## Hitler's Horoscope

In the late 1930s, astrologer Wilhelm Wulff was ordered by Nazi officials to make predictions that would help Germany fight World War II. However, as Wulff writes in *Zodiac and Swastika*, the 1940 horoscope of Nazi leader Adolf Hitler showed that the dictator was doomed. After the horoscope was cast, Hitler survived an assassination attempt and committed suicide in 1945 with his wife Eva Braun; his body was never recovered. Wulff's predictions therefore seem uncannily accurate if they were actually made at the time the astrologer claims:

I have been studying Hitler's horoscope. . . . I have a pretty clear idea of what is ultimately in store for him. He will probably die under the hand of an assassin, certainly in "Neptunian"— that is, enigmatic—circumstances, in which a woman will play a leading part. The world will probably never know the precise details of his death, for in Hitler's horoscope Neptune has long been in bad aspect to other planets. Moreover, Neptune is extremely strong in his horoscope, and it was always to be expected that his great military projects would have a dubious outcome.

*In 1956 astrologer Jeane Dixon predicted that a Democrat would win the presidential election in 1960, and that this president would die in office.*

Action must be taken quickly if Germany is to be spared even greater misfortunes."[70] Schellenberg failed to act, but Wulff's predictions came true. Germany was defeated, the Nazis were destroyed in May 1945, and the United States and the Soviet Union soon became great superpowers, just as the astrologer had divined.

## The Jeane Dixon Effect

Wulff gives the impression that 100 percent of his predictions were accurate, but his book does not cover forecasts that did not come true. This is typical in many cases concerning astrological prognostications—accurate forecasts are long remembered while incorrect predictions are quickly forgotten. This phenomenon even has a name, the *Jeane Dixon effect*, named after the woman who was a leading psychic and astrologer from the 1960s until her death in 1997.

Dixon is best known for her predictions concerning President John F. Kennedy. In 1956, *Parade* magazine reported: "As for the 1960 election Mrs. Dixon thinks it will be . . . won by a Democrat. He will be assassinated or die in office though not necessarily in his first term."[71] Kennedy did indeed win the election, and in June 1963, a year before the end of his term, Dixon elaborated on her earlier prediction, saying, "I still see a large coffin being carried into the White House. This means that the President will meet death elsewhere and his body will be returned there for national mourning."[72]

Five months later, when the president was killed in Dallas, Texas, on November 22, Dixon became a national celebrity as many in the media touted her seemingly astonishingly accurate prediction. Forgotten was the fact that three years earlier, in the summer of 1960, Dixon had predicted that Richard Nixon, Kennedy's Republican opponent, would win the White House instead of Kennedy. Skeptics also point out that Kennedy had about a 28 percent chance of dying in office due to unfortunate historical precedents. In the century before Kennedy's murder, three out of eighteen presidents were assassinated (Abraham Lincoln, James Garfield, and William McKinley), and two more died in office (Warren G. Harding and Franklin D. Roosevelt). Given these statistics, Dixon's forecast had nearly a one in three chance of coming true.

Whatever the case, in the 1960s, Dixon became the leading astrologer in the United States. Every year, between Christmas and New Year's Eve, she made predictions for the coming year. Many of these prognostications, which appeared in national magazines, were inaccurate.

*Commuters read newspaper accounts of President John F. Kennedy's assassination, an event that astrologer Jeane Dixon had foretold in astonishingly accurate detail.*

For example, in 1967, Dixon stated that the Soviet Union would beat the United States in the race to the moon and that World War III would soon begin. She also predicted that a cure for cancer could be discovered that year. In later years, Dixon incorrectly predicted that actor Alec Baldwin would become terribly ill in 1997, and comedian Ellen De-Generes would be arrested by the Secret Service when she crashed the presidential inauguration in 1998. Despite her poor record, when the astrologer died in 1997, many newspaper obituaries cited only her amazing forecasts concerning Kennedy. Commenting on this phenomenon, Todd Carroll writes on Skeptics.com that the Jeane Dixon effect reveals "the tendency of the mass media to hype or exaggerate a few correct predictions by [an astrologer], guaranteeing that they will be remembered, while forgetting or ignoring the much more numerous incorrect predictions."[73]

## Stocks and Planets

Whenever astrologers fail to predict the future, some claim that they cannot calculate specific events, just broad trends. Others say that they can forecast large events, but not the small incidents of daily life. Skeptics say if this is true, astrologers should be able to use their knowledge of coming trends to become incredibly wealthy. As Fraknoi writes, "Astrologers could amass billions by forecasting general stock-market behavior or commodity futures, and thus not have to charge their clients high fees. In October, 1987, how many astrologers actually foresaw Black Monday when the stock market took such a large tumble and warned their clients about it?"[74]

As it happens, however, there have been astrologers who have predicted trends in the stock market, even the Black Monday stock crash. One of them, Evangeline Adams, worked for the most famous speculator in the twentieth century, John Pierpont (J.P.) Morgan. In 1901,

# Evangeline Adams

Evangeline Adams, born February 8, 1868, was America's most famous astrologer in the early decades of the twentieth century. After successfully predicting a spectacular New York hotel fire, she became enormously popular through her syndicated astrology columns and her radio show, which was broadcast three times a week. The story of her professional success is described by Karen Christino on the Online College of Astrology Web site:

*Evangeline Adams gained fame as an astrologer in the early twentieth century.*

[Evangeline] Adams had the strong Uranus and Aquarius placements found in so many astrologer's charts, as well as many placements in the intuitive sign of Pisces. From her New York City studios in Carnegie Hall, Adams served an exclusive clientele. She popularized astrology through her four books and 1931 radio show, making the general public aware of astrology as an important topic of study for the first time. Adams claimed to have predicted the famous Windsor Hotel fire in 1899, one of the worst disasters the city had yet seen. She was tried in a New York City court [after being arrested for] fortune-telling in 1914, but was found not-guilty, with the judge stating that she raised astrology "to the dignity of an exact science." Adams . . . helped men like J.P. Morgan and Charles Schwab amass their vast fortunes, and, indeed, she had forecast not only the stock market crash of 1929 but also the United States' involvement in World War II.

Morgan was the wealthiest man in the world, having built his fortune through banking and investment—and he often consulted with Adams, granddaughter of President John Quincy Adams, before investing. Purportedly Adams's advice enabled Morgan's personal wealth to grow to $22 billion—about $220 billion in today's dollars, or five times the wealth of the world's richest man, Bill Gates.

When a reporter told Morgan that most millionaires would be reluctant to use astrology to play the stock market, Morgan gave his famous reply, "Millionaires don't hire astrologers, billionaires do."[75]

To create planetary predictions for the stock market, astrologers work in several ways. They might use the birth time of a president or chief executive officer of a corporation or make the forecast based on the incorporation date of a specific company. The selected date is compared with progressions and transits. If the aspects are harmonious, it is believed to be a good time to buy stock in that company. If omens are bad, the investor is told not to invest or to sell off the company's stock. Astrologer Joni Patry offers some general predictions:

> If the Sun is in hard aspect (square) to Uranus, the stock will tend to fluctuate. Connections between the natal Sun (of the company or CEO) and Pluto symbolize a powerful mover on the [stock] exchange. Its price fluctuation will affect the whole industry.

*Astrologers say that they can predict the rise and fall of stocks, such as those traded on the New York Stock Exchange.*

The Moon represents the public or masses. . . . Transits to the Moon can cause erratic trading patterns. Natal charts with Moon/Uranus connections cause irregular price movements. Moon/Saturn connections bring stability. . . . Saturn will lower the price of a stock as it passes over planets.[76]

## Wall Street's Best-Known Astrologer

Technical analyst Arch Crawford has gained attention because he uses astrology to predict movements on the stock market. Crawford, who began working for top Wall Street firms in the early 1960s, conducted extensive research into astrological phenomena. Like astrologers from ancient Babylon, he analyzed planetary aspects and transits along with astrophysical events such as sunspots, tides, and volcanic activity. By doing so, Crawford found he could correlate astrological and astrophysical information to negative or positive prices on the stock market.

Crawford's specialty is called market timing, a controversial strategy of buying or selling a stock by attempting to predict its future price. Most market timers base their analyses on economic conditions or the possibility of events such as war. Crawford, however, bases his predictions on daily astrological events. On the Web site "Arch Crawford's Perspectives," Crawford explains how he developed his technique:

I tracked the ups and downs of the [New York Stock Exchange] from 1897 through 1970 and correlated them with planetary movements and configurations. I could see that the correlating reliability factor ran very high—far above chance expectation. The only sensible conclusion was that various planetary arrangements disrupted the normally expected drift of the [stock market], sometimes very dramatically.

The same is true, for example, in the copper, gold and futures markets.[77]

In 1977, Crawford began selling this information in a newsletter, *Crawford Perspectives*. Unlike most market-timing newsletters that use technical business jargon, *Crawford Perspectives* is filled with astrological terms. It includes a list of "Key Astronomic Activity" that provides an analysis of astrological phenomena predicted to affect the stock market in the future. During the first four years of the newsletter's existence, the stock timer was correct an incredible 90 percent of the time. Since then, Crawford's market predictions have remained among the most accurate in Wall Street history.

Among approximately one thousand market-timing newsletters, *Crawford Perspectives* is but one of the few that relies on astrology. Even as skeptics try to debunk astrological prediction as superstition, Crawford was rated as the number one stock timer several years in a row by the prestigious *Timer Digest*, a watchdog publication that analyzes the accuracy of timer newsletters. Crawford's long-term record places him in the top ten of all market timers since the late 1970s. However, Crawford has been derided for relying on astrology despite his accuracy. For example, a 1988 article in *Barron's* referred to him not as an incredibly accurate market timer but "Wall Street's Best Known Astrologer."[78]

## The Crash of 1987

Crawford's analysis is based on the age-old belief that celestial episodes are connected to events on earth. For example, during the planetary alignment known as the Harmonic Convergence in August 1987, Crawford warned that this celestial event would signal the end of the long-term bull market, characterized by rising prices. In his August 8 newsletter, stating that a horrendous crash

would occur in the coming weeks, Crawford told investors his "long-term sell signal is set in stone" and they should sell "everything by August the 24."[19]

Crawford's prediction was immediately mocked in several influential publications, including the *Wall Street Journal*. The laughing stopped, however, when the market timer's words came true. The long bull market reached its peak on August 25, and stocks slipped continually until the infamous crash of October 19, when the market fell 508 points and lost a record 23 percent of its value. While this was not exactly a harmonic event as far as financiers were concerned, astrologers claimed that the convergence of the planets influenced human behavior and caused the crash.

*Traders watch monitors as the October 1987 stock market crash becomes reality. Analyst Arch Crawford had predicted this crash based on astrological signs.*

Skeptics argued that Crawford's prediction was actually a self-fulfilling prophecy. That is, when he advised his clients to sell everything, he created a panic in the already volatile stock market. As skittish investors saw Crawford's customers selling, they too sold their stocks, causing prices to drop as millions of shares flooded the market. Some say that if Crawford had predicted the opposite—that prices would rise and customers should buy—the market would not have seen the sharp downturn.

Such is the nature of speculation and astrological market timing. Whether or not the market timer contributed to the crash, he convinced many that his methods were solid, and his customer base has grown. Crawford continues to publish his newsletter but he cautions, "In market trading . . . nothing works all of the time, and future results can't be guaranteed. But planetary pattern disruptions can't be dismissed, and it makes sense to increase a refined understanding of them."[80]

## Debate Continues

Despite the success of Crawford and other astrologers, many remain unconvinced of the powers of the prognosticators. Meanwhile, scientists continue to conduct research into the accuracy of the stargazers. One study from the mid-1970s tracked three thousand published predictions of well-known astrologers for five years. Out of all the specific predictions about politicians, celebrities, and athletes, only about 10 percent came to pass. Those who conducted the study noted that astute reporters or even someone who followed the news closely would probably have an equal or better record of accuracy.

Since astrology is by far the most popular method of prognostication used today, the debate about its precision will continue. As to when the debate will end, perhaps the answer is written in the stars.

# Notes

## Introduction: The Planetary Rhythms

1. H.J. Eysenck and D.K.B. Nias, *Astrology: Science or Superstition?* New York: St. Martin's, 1982, p. vii.

2. Bart J. Bok and Lawrence E. Jerome, *Objections to Astrology.* Buffalo, NY: Prometheus, 1975, p. 10.

3. Quoted in Michael Gilleland, "Horace, Ode 1.11," Horace, Ode 1.11 (no date). www.merriampark.com/horcarm111. htm.

## Chapter 1: The Mysterious Elements of Astrology

4. Peter Whitfield, *Astrology: A History.* New York: Harry N. Abrams, 2001, p. 10.

5. Quoted in Whitfield, *Astrology*, p. 12.

6. Quoted in Whitfield, *Astrology*, p. 26.

7. Quoted in Whitfield, *Astrology*, p. 24.

8. Claudius Ptolemy, *Tetrabiblios*, University of Chicago, April 13, 2005. http://pene lope.uchicago.edu/Thayer/E/Roman/ Texts/Ptolemy/Tetrabiblos/1A*.html#1.

9. Dan Sewell Ward, "Science Versus Astrology," halexandria.org, 2003. www.halexandria.org/dward330.htm.

10. Roger B. Culver and Philip A. Ianna, *Astrology: True or False?* Buffalo, NY: Prometheus, 1988, pp. 53–54.

11. Linda Goodman, *Linda Goodman's Sun Signs.* New York: Bantam, 1968, p. xviii.

12. Fred Gettings, *The Book of the Zodiac.* London: Triune, 1972, p. 121.

13. Culver and Ianna, *Astrology*, p. 125.

14. Saffi Crawford and Geraldine Sullivan, *The Power of Birthdays, Stars, & Numbers.* New York: Ballantine, 1998, p. 13.

15. Llewellyn George, *The New A to Z Horoscope Maker and Delineator.* St. Paul, MN: Llewellyn, 1987, p. 221.

16. Andrew Fraknoi, "The Universe at Your Fingertips Activity: Activities with Astrology," 2005. www.astrosociety.org/ education/astro/act3/astrology3.html# defense.

17. Robert Todd Carroll, "Astrology," The Skeptic's Dictionary, 2000. http://skepdic. com/iching.html.

## Chapter 2: Astrology, Personality, and Health

18. Frances Sakoian and Louis S. Acker, *The Astrologer's Handbook.* New York: Harper & Row, 1973, p. 103.

19. Sakoian and Acker, *The Astrologer's Handbook*, p. 331.

20. Eysenck and Nias, *Astrology*, p. 35.

21. Michel Gauquelin, "Is There Really a Mars Effect?," Environmental Cosmology, 2005. www.encosm.net/mars_effect.htm.

22. Eysenck and Nias, *Astrology*, p. 201.

23. Quoted in Bok and Jerome, *Objections to Astrology*, pp. 9–10.

24. Gauquelin, "Is There Really a Mars Effect?"

25. Quoted in J.W. Nienhuys, "Review of *The 'Mars Effect': A French Test of 1,000 Sports Champions*," Planetos, 2003. www.planetos.info/marsfxre.html.

26. J.T. Ford, *Zodiac Manager*. Franklin Lakes, NJ: Career Press, 2003, p. 6.

27. Quoted in William Sluis, "Jenrette," *Lubbock Avalanche-Journal*, 1997. www.lubbockonline.com/news/073197/jenrette.htm.

28. Teri King, *Business, Success and Astrology*. New York: St. Martin's, 1974, pp. 24–25.

29. Quoted in Sluis, "Jenrette."

30. Yaschpaule, "Astrology, Hand Analysis, Management Science and Business Prospects," Asia Pacific Management Forum, 1998. www.apmforum.com/review/asiafeature2.htm.

31. Yaschpaule, "Astrology, Hand Analysis, Management Science and Business Prospects."

32. Bob Steiner, "Astrology Is Bigotry," Pac-c.org, 2004. www.pac-c.org/astrology2.htm.

33. Terry Lamb, *Born to Be Together*. Carlsbad, CA: Hay House, 1998, p. 50.

34. Lamb, *Born to Be Together*, p. 134.

35. Lamb, *Born to Be Together*, p. 129.

36. Marilyn, "Marilyn's Astrology," Kent State University. www.personal.kent.edu/~msmiller.

37. Adele Lang & Susi Rajah, *How to Spot a Bastard by His Sun Sign*. New York: Thomas Dunne, 2002, p. 3.

38. Goodman, *Linda Goodman's Star Signs*, p. 37.

39. Goodman, *Linda Goodman's Star Signs*, p. 37.

40. *Times of India*, "Astrology is Rubbish, Says New Research," August 2003. www.rickross.com/reference/general/general574.html.

41. Fraknoi, "The Universe at Your Fingertips Activity."

## Chapter 3: Astrology's Influence on Daily Events

42. Holly Mathis, "Astrological Forecast," *Los Angeles Times*, October 20, 2005, p. H1.

43. Quoted in Mathis, "Astrological Forecast," p. H1.

44. Sakoian and Acker, *The Astrologer's Handbook*, p. 120.

45. Quoted in Philip Plait, *Bad Astronomy*. New York: John Wiley & Sons, 2002, p. 214.

46. Plait, *Bad Astronomy*, p. 214.

47. Ellen McCaffery, *Astrology: Its History and Influence in the Western World*. New York: Samuel Weiser, 1970, p. 45.

48. John Anthony West and Jan Gerhard Toonder, *The Case for Astrology*. New York: Coward-McCann, 1970, p. 14.

49. Quoted in D. Trull, "Nancy's Star-Crossed Secret," *ParaScope*, 1997. www.parascope.com/articles/0497/reagan03.htm.

50. Quoted in Julie N. Lynem, "The Sage of Aquarius: S.F. Company Says What You Don't Know About Astrology Can Be Harmful to Your Business' Health," *San Francisco Chronicle*, October 27, 2002. www.sfgate.com/cgi-bin/article.cgi?file=/chronicle/archive/2002/10/27/BU169447.DTL&type=business.

51. Jack Fertig, "Fraknoi's Complaint," AOL Hometown. http://members.aol.com/jackfertig/fraknois10.htm.

52. Quoted in VEDA—Vedas and Vedic Knowledge Online, "Veda," 2005. www.veda.harekrsna.cz/encyclopedia/general.htm#12.

53. Quoted in Marion D. March (ed.), *Millennium: Fears, Fantasies & Facts: Astrologers Predict 2000*. San Diego: ACS, 1998, pp. 89–90.

54. Quoted in March, *Millennium*, p. 90.

55. souledout.org, "The Transition of Ages—Pisces to Aquarius," 2004. www.souledout.org/cosmology/ages/transitionages.html.

56. E. Alan Meece, "Prospects for a Golden Age: The Meaning of the Great Planetary Cycles," california.com, 1996. www.california.com/~eameece/prospect.htm#WHAT%20ABOUT%20THAT%20AGE%20OF%20AQUARIUS?

57. Quoted in March, *Millennium*, p. 109.

58. Meece, "Prospects for a Golden Age."

59. Liz Greene, "The Terrorist Attack on America: An Astrological Perspective," astro.com, September 15, 2001. www.astro.com/h/wtc_e.htm.

60. Greene, "The Terrorist Attack on America."

61. Greene, "The Terrorist Attack on America."

## Chapter 4: Forecasting and Transforming the Future

62. Quoted in *Crawford Perspectives*, "More About Arch Crawford," 2005. www.crawfordperspectives.com/fate_detectives.html.

63. R. Campbell Thompson, *The Reports of Magicians and Astrologers*. New York: AMS, 1977, p. xv.

64. Ray T. Marlbrough, *Charms, Spells & Formulas*. St. Paul, MN: Llewellyn, 1985, pp. 8–9.

65. Quoted in Christopher Warnock, "Planetary Hour Elections in the *Key of Solomon*," Renaissance Astrology, 2001. www.renaissanceastrology.com/hours keysolomonarticle.html.

66. Quoted in Warnock, "Planetary Hour Elections in the *Key of Solomon*."

67. Quoted in World-Mysteries.com, "Michel Nostradamus," 2005. www.world-mysteries.com/awr_5.htm.

68. Quoted in Edgar Leoni, *Nostradamus and His Prophecies*. New York: Bell, 1982, p. 309.

69. Will McWhorter, "Nostradamus: Predictions for the Past, Present and Future," Homepage of Will McWhorter, April 29, 1993. http://boisdarc.tamu-commerce.edu/www/w/willmc/nostra.htm.

70. Wulff, *Zodiac and Swastika*. New York: Coward, McCann & Geoghegan, 1973, p. 97.

71. Quoted in Todd Carroll, "Jeane Dixon & the Jeane Dixon Effect," Skeptics.com, 2005. http://skepdic.com/dixon.html.

72. Quoted in Ruth Montgomery, *A Gift of Prophecy: The Phenomenal Jeane Dixon*. New York: William Morrow, 1965, p. 7.

73. Todd Carroll, "Jeane Dixon & the Jeane Dixon Effect."

74. Fraknoi, "The Universe at Your Fingertips Activity."

75. Quoted in Yaschpaule, "Astrology, Hand Analysis, Management Science and Business Prospects," Asia Pacific Management Forum, 1998. www.apm forum.com/review/asiafeature2.htm.

76. Joni Patry, "Planetary Stock Trading," Galactic Center, 2004. www.galactic center.org/astrology_stock_trading.htm.

77. *Crawford Perspectives*, "More About Arch Crawford."

78. Quoted in *Crawford Perspectives*, "More About Arch Crawford."

79. Quoted in *Crawford Perspectives*, "More About Arch Crawford."

80. *Crawford Perspectives*, "More About Arch Crawford."

# For Further Reading

## Books

Page Bryant, *Star Magic*. Jackson, TN: Dragonhawk, 2002. A young person's guide to magic and astrology based on New Age concepts.

Madeline Gerwick-Brodeur and Lisa Lenard, *The Complete Idiot's Guide to Astrology*. Indianapolis, IN: Alpha, 2003. A comprehensive exploration of stargazing written in an amusing and easy-to-understand style.

Julia Marsden, *Scope Out Your Life: What Your Sign Says About You*. New York: Scholastic, 1999. A book that examines the alleged links between the zodiac and specific personality traits.

Georgia Routsis Savas, *Total Astrology: What the Stars Say About Life and Love*. New York: HarperCollins, 2000. The astrological influences of the stars and planets and their purported effects on daily life and future events.

Maria Shaw, *Maria Shaw's Star Gazer: Your Soul Searching, Dream Seeking, Make Something Happen Guide to the Future*. St. Paul, MN: Llewellyn, 2003. A New Age book that advises readers on ways they can shape their lives by using astrological data.

## Web Sites

"Astrolabe," 2005, http:alabe.com/freechart. A site that offers a free astrology chart and chart-making software to users who input their dates, times, and places of birth.

astrology.com, "Daily Teen Horoscopes," 2005. http://horoscopes.astrology.com/index/dailyteenindex.html. A Web site with daily advice and future predictions based on astrology.

3 Muses, "Zodiac Girlz," October 23, 2005. www.zodiacgirlz.com/news.html. A site that includes daily horoscopes, compatibility advice, and astrology-based games, fashion, greetings, and links.

# Works Consulted

## Books

Bart J. Bok and Lawrence E. Jerome, *Objections to Astrology*. Buffalo: Prometheus, 1975. A book signed by 192 of the world's leading scientists that offers a wide range of criticism concerning theories and beliefs about astrological divination.

Saffi Crawford and Geraldine Sullivan, *The Power of Birthdays, Stars, & Numbers*. New York: Ballantine, 1998. Two astrologers list 365 personality traits, career strengths, and tips on love for individual birthdays.

Roger B. Culver and Philip A. Ianna, *Astrology: True or False?* Buffalo, NY: Prometheus, 1988. A scientific discussion of astronomy, physics, the history of the universe, and their relationship to the ancient art of astrology.

H.J. Eysenck and D.K.B. Nias, *Astrology: Science or Superstition*? New York: St. Martin's, 1982. A skeptical inquiry into the pseudoscience of astrology in which the authors use scientific reasoning to dismiss many commonly held beliefs about the predictive system.

J.T. Ford, *Zodiac Manager*. Franklin Lakes, NJ: The Career Press, 2003. A book that claims that a person can advance his or her career by using astrology to figure out the personal characteristics of managers, co-workers, and bosses.

Eurenio Garin, *Astrology in the Renaissance*. London: Routledge & Kegan Paul, 1976. First published in Italy, this scholarly work explores the important role astrology played in the fifteenth and sixteenth centuries when it was revived and popularized by Renaissance philosophers.

Llewellyn George, *The New A to Z Horoscope Maker and Delineator*. St. Paul: Llewellyn, 1987. A best-selling guide to astrology with detailed information that allows the reader to construct and interpret horoscopes.

Fred Gettings, *The Book of the Zodiac*. London: Triune, 1972. Detailed descriptions of traits associated with each astrological sign, illustrated with ancient drawings and paintings.

Linda Goodman, *Linda Goodman's Star Signs*. New York: St. Martin's Griffin, 1987. With over one million copies in print, this book purports to help people improve their lives, relationships, and businesses by consulting the stars.

Linda Goodman, *Linda Goodman's Sun Signs*. New York: Bantam, 1968. A book about birth-sign astrology with details about how people's sun signs allegedly affect their careers, romantic possibilities, and other aspects of life.

Teri King, *Business, Success and Astrology*. New York: St. Martin's, 1974. A book that advises people about methods they can use to their benefit in the workplace applying astrological analysis of personality characteristics to bosses, coworkers, partners, and clients.

Terry Lamb, *Born to Be Together*. Carlsbad, CA: Hay House, 1998. A book that uses astrology as a guide to help readers solve problems concerning love, romance, and relationships.

Adele Lang and Susi Rajah, *How to Spot a Bastard by His Sun Sign*. New York: Thomas Dunne, 2002. A harshly critical book that emphasizes the negative personal characteristics of each sign as a way to help women avoid negative personality types.

Edgar Leoni, *Nostradamus and His Prophecies*. New York: Bell, 1982. A biography of one of history's most famous soothsayers, along with the complete version of his *Centuries* in both English and the original languages.

Grant Lewi, *Heaven Knows What*. St. Paul, MN: Llewellyn, 1987. A how-to book on astrology with instructions on casting and interpreting complete natal charts.

Marion D. March (ed.), *Millennium: Fears, Fantasies & Facts: Astrologists Predict 2000*. San Diego: ACS, 1998. A book with mostly inaccurate astrological predictions for the early years of the twenty-first century.

Ray T. Marlbrough, *Charms, Spells & Formulas*. St. Paul, MN: Llewellyn, 1985. A guide to casting spells, with instructions on making gris-gris, herb candles, doll magic, incense, oils, and powders, written by a New Orleans hoodoo doctor.

Ellen McCaffery, *Astrology: Its History and Influence in the Western World*. New York: Samuel Weiser, 1970. An account of astrology from the times of ancient Babylon through the Renaissance and into the twentieth century.

Ruth Montgomery, *A Gift of Prophecy: The Phenomenal Jeane Dixon*. New York: William Morrow, 1965. A best-selling account of a woman whose predictions were sought by the public and presidents alike.

Philip Plait, *Bad Astronomy*. New York: John Wiley & Sons, 2002. Part of the Bad Science series, this book debunks myths, legends, and misconceptions about astronomy, including those that deal with astrology.

Frances Sakoian and Louis S. Acker, *The Astrologer's Handbook*. New York: Harper & Row, 1973. A guide that interprets the horoscope with descriptions, characteristics, and advice geared toward each individual planet, sign, house, and aspect of a natal chart.

R. Campbell Thompson, *The Reports of Magicians and Astrologers*. New York: AMS, 1977. Originally printed in London in 1900, this book contains hundreds of astrological predictions translated from ancient Assyrian tablets.

John Anthony West and Jan Gerhard Toonder, *The Case for Astrology*. New York: Coward-McCann, 1970. A book that mixes historic examples of astrological prediction with complicated and obscure metaphysical jargon that purportedly proves the accuracy of astrology.

Peter Whitfield, *Astrology: A History*. New York: Harry N. Abrams, 2001. A study that emphasizes the ancient philosophical, intellectual, and religious significance of astrology among those who developed the belief system.

Wilhelm Wulff, *Zodiac and Swastika*. New York: Coward, McCann & Geoghegan, 1973. The astonishing story of a German astrologer who claims he was recruited into the Nazi cause against his will and forced to cast horoscopes and predict the future for Adolf Hitler and his top officials.

## Periodicals

Holly Mathis, "Astrological Forecast," *Los Angeles Times*, October 20, 2005.

## Internet Sources

Robert Todd Carroll, "Astrology," The Skeptics.com, 2000. http://skepdic.com/iching.html.

Todd Carroll, "Jeane Dixon & the Jeane Dixon Effect," Skeptics.com, 2005. http://skepdic.com/dixon.html.

Karen Christino, "Evangeline Adams' Horary Technique," Online College of Astrology, 2002. www.astrocollege.com/campus/librar ies/Evangeline_Adams_Horary_Technique .pdf#search='J.P.%20Morgan%20evan geline%20adams.

*Crawford Perspectives*, "More About Arch Crawford," 2005. www.crawfordperspec tives.com/fate_detectives.html.

David Emery, "Rumor Watch: Terrorist Attack on U.S." Urban Legends and Folklore. http://urbanlegends.about.com/library/weekly/aa091101b.htm.

Jack Fertig, "Fraknoi's Complaint," AOL Hometown. http://members.aol.com/jack fertig/fraknois10.htm.

Andrew Fraknoi, "The Universe at Your Fingertips Activity: Activities with Astrology," 2005. www.astrosociety.org/educa tion/astro/act3/astrology3.html#defense.

Michel Gauquelin, "Is There Really a Mars Effect?" Environmental Cosmology, 2005. www.encosm.net/mars_effect.htm.

Michael Gilleland, "Horace, Ode 1.11," Horace, Ode 1.11 (no date). www.merriampark.com/horcarm111.htm.

Liz Greene, "The Terrorist Attack on America: An Astrological Perspective," astro.com, September 15, 2001. www.astro.com/h/wtc_e.htm.

Julie N. Lynem, "The Sage of Aquarius: S.F. Company Says What You Don't Know About Astrology Can Be Harmful to Your Business' Health," *San Francisco Chronicle*, October 27, 2002. www.sfgate.com/cgi-bin/article.cgi?file=/chronicle/archive/2002/10/27/BU169447.DTL&type=business.

Marilyn, "Marilyn's Astrology," Kent State University, (no date). www.personal.kent.edu/~msmiller.

Will McWhorter, "Nostradamus: Predictions for the Past, Present and Future," Homepage of Will McWhorter, April 29, 1993. http://boisdarc.tamu-commerce.edu/www/w/willmc/nostra.htm.

E. Alan Meece, "Prospects for a Golden Age: The Meaning of the Great Planetary Cycles," california.com, 1996. www.california.com/~eameece/prospect.htm#WHAT%20ABOUT%20THAT%20AGE%20OF%20AQUARIUS?

Richard Alan Miller, "Planetary Hours," Northwest Botanicals, 1993. www.nwbotanicals.org/oak/magick/planetaryhours.htm.

J. W. Nienhuys, "Review of *The 'Mars Effect': A French Test of 1,000 Sports Champions*," Planetos, 2003. www.planetos.info/marsfxre.html.

Joni Patry, "Planetary Stock Trading," Galactic Center, 2004. www.galacticcenter.org/astrology_stock_trading.htm.

Claudius Ptolemy, *Tetrabiblios*, University of Chicago, April 18, 2005. http://penelope.uchicago.edu/Thayer/E/Roman/Texts/Ptolemy/Tetrabiblos/home.html.

Claudius Ptolemy, *Tetrabiblios*, University of Chicago, April 13, 2005. http://penelope.uchicago.edu/Thayer/E/Roman/Texts/Ptolemy/Tetrabiblos/1A*.html#1.

James Randi, "Commentary," James Randi Educational Foundation, June 15, 2001. www.randi.org/jr/06-15-01.html.

Rosicrucian Fellowship, "The Aquarian Age," 2003. www.rosicrucian.com/zineen/magen119.htm.

William Sluis, "Jenrette," *Lubbock Avalanche-Journal*, 1997. www.lubbockonline.com/news/073197/jenrette.htm.

Bob Steiner, "Astrology Is Bigotry," Pac-c.org, 2004. www.pac-c.org/astrology2.htm.

"The Transition of Ages—Pisces to Aquarius," souledout.org, 2004, www.souledout.org/cosmology/ages/transitionages.html.

*Times of India*, "Astrology is Rubbish, Says New *Research*," August 2003. www.rickross.com/reference/general/general574.html.

D. Trull, "Nancy's Star-Crossed Secret," *parascope.com*, 1997. www.parascope.com/articles/0497/reagan02.htm.

D. Trull, "So Speaks the Soothsayer," *parascope.com*, 1997. www.parascope.com/articles/0497/reagan03.htm.

Dan Sewell Ward, "Science Versus Astrology," halexandria.org, 2003. www.halexandria.org/dward330.htm.

VEDA—Vedas and Vedic Knowledge Online, "Veda," 2005. www.veda.harekrsna.cz/encyclopedia/general.htm#12.

Christopher Warnock, "Planetary Hour Elections in the *Key of Solomon*," Renaissance Astrology, 2001. www.renaissanceastrology.com/hourskeysolomonarticle.html.

World-Mysteries.com, "Michel Nostradamus," 2005. www.world-mysteries.com/awr_5.htm.

Yaschpaule, "Astrology, Hand Analysis, Management Science and Business Prospects," Asia Pacific Management Forum, 1998. www.apmforum.com/review/asiafeature2.htm.

# Index

# Picture Credits

Cover photo: Signs of the Zodiac, detail from the ceiling of the Sala dello Zodiaco, 1579 (fresco), Costa, Lorenzo the Younger (Mantovano) (1537-1583)/Palazzo Ducale, Mantua, Italy, Alinari/Bridgeman Art Library

Maury Aaseng, 35

Mike Agliolo/Science Photo Library/Photo Researchers, Inc., 67

AP/Wide World Photos, 8, 64, 88

© Bettmann/CORBIS, 83, 91, 92, 94

© Bildarchiv Monheim GmbH/Alamy, 16

© Noiriko and Don Carroll/Alamy, 22

© Condé Nast Archive/CORBIS, 44

Araldo de Luca/CORBIS, 29

Sebastian D'Souza/AFP/Getty Images, 20

© Bob Elam/Alamy, 48

Mike Evens/AFP/Getty Images, 61

Hulton Archive/Getty Images, 9, 19, 84

Tony Korody/Time Life Pictures/Getty Images, 62

© Lake County Museum/CORBIS, 68

Erich Lessing/Art Resource, NY, 13

Library of Congress, 86

Mary Evans Picture Library, 12

© Mediscan/CORBIS, 53

Carl Mydans/Time Life Pictures/Getty Images, 89

NASA Jet Propulsion Laboratory (NASA-JPL), 33

The National Portrait Gallery, 25 (large image)

PhotoDisc, 39, 57

© Roger Ressmeyer/CORBIS, 73

© Reuters/CORBIS, 74, 78

Jeffery Allan Salter/CORBIS, 36

Nancy R. Schiff/Hulton Archive/Getty Images, 43

© Denis Scott/CORBIS, 25 (inset)

© Stapleton Collection/CORBIS, 7, 15

© Simon Taplin/CORBIS, 56

# About the Author

Stuart A. Kallen is the author of more than two hundred nonfiction books for children and young adults. He has written on topics ranging from the theory of relativity to the history of rock and roll. In addition, Mr. Kallen has written award-winning children's videos and television scripts. In his spare time, he is a singer/songwriter/guitarist in San Diego, California.